W9-CPB-862

These Walk On Water

the gospel with power

Returning the church to the destiny God intended

Danny Steyne

Forewords by Randy Clark

&

Rolland & Heidi Baker

Published by MOW Books

mow

"...another book about what Jesus did..."
John 21:25

These Walk On Water
Copyright ©2007 by Danny Steyne

Scripture references are taken from the Holy Bible, New International Version Copyright © 1973, 1978, 1984 International Bible Society, Colorado Springs, Colorado

Published by:

MOWBooks
P.O. Box 212204
Columbia SC 29221-2204
www.MountainOfWorship.com
worship@MountainOfWorship.com
803-665-8990

MOWBooks is a ministry of Mountain Of Worship, a South Carolina non-profit organization dedicated to perpetuate the event of sustained, perpetual lifestyle worship of Jesus that releases a heavenly demonstration that causes the lost to bow their knee and the found to adore the One they live for ... until every knee bows ... until every tongue tells ... both the lost and the found ... in heaven and in hell ... that JESUS is Lord!

ISBN 1-59872-715-X

Printed in the United States of America
For Worldwide Distribution

Dedication

They have been my witness and my inspiration to follow hard after God. They have refined my beliefs, and have demonstrated that God is not confined to the great and powerful. They are the ones that have brought reality to the religious thinking in me, proving the total ineffectiveness of a system void of power. They have had dreams and visions, sometimes broken, always bigger than themselves. They have asked me the hard questions about my love for God, without wondering if that was sacrilegious or not. My failure to follow after God directly affects their ability to see God move, not that I am anything, but simply that they watch with eyes that wonder and trust.

I'm simply a father to Jenni, Peter, Vanessa, Davey, Jackie, Christy, Abby, Rea and Elijah. I'm just a man, whom God has called to demonstrate, educate, and impart the purposes of God to a generation... their generation and others along with them. They embody the hope of this book. They are the generation of the righteous. They have pointed me towards a God who invites us all to walk on water, rather than simply living through storms. I have watched each of them walk through their own valleys, their own fires, their own floods... I am amazed at all the ways God has brought them through, and know that I will be amazed in years to come too!

My Children, I dedicate this volume to you... may you be the generation that will "walk on water" and release the Kingdom to this earth in ways that astound all! May you be the generation that asks the question, "Where is the Lord God of Elijah?" May you be the generation that knows the value of crying out to God as you "... remember those days of old when Moses, God's servant, led his people out of Egypt, and they cried out, "Where is the One who brought Israel through the sea, with Moses as their shepherd? Where is the God who sent his Holy Spirit to be among his people?" (Isaiah 63:11 TLB) My Children, cry out... and then walk on water!

Acknowledgments

Years ago my parents, Phil & Jeanne Steyne, handed me a baton. They gave their lives to the nations.... doing all they knew to do to reach the generation that was theirs to reach! They loved passionately, often extravagantly to the Kingdom in both time and resource. The hope they held was for unprecedented harvest. Their consistent, powerful love of Jesus has always been a blessing to my life! They continue to pursue that even in their eighties! May they see the fruit of their vision! My Dad once gave me precious wisdom after hearing an "eloquent" sermon I had just finished preaching. He said, "Danny, always put the cookies on the bottom shelf so everyone can get them!" My prayer is that this book will be easily understood by all, and that the demonstration of His Kingdom will flow easily through your life as a result.

My greatest thanks always goes to the one God has called beside me. Karen has been such a blessing to me as I write, spending hours on a computer, while she carries the weight of a home and many children. She also, unlike so many, has understood the value of pursuing our King and His Vision together. She knows that we were destined to reach the nations and that part of that involves sacrifice. She, in apostolic love, has laid down her life for Jesus, demonstrating His intense Love to me on a daily basis. I treasure you Karen...

I would be remiss if I did not mention those other valiant servants who continue to draw me into a greater a deeper love of Jesus every day. Rolland & Heidi Baker; you are true friends and have had such a profound impact on my life... more than that you showed me this laid down love. Randy Clark; a great friend and one who carries a blazing torch that has set me on fire. Bob & Bonnie Jones; what a precious love you pour into us with such revelatory precision. Surprise "Supressa" Sithole; you carry the marks of Jesus on you... His joy, His friendship, His love... I love you my brother! Jim Reilly... my comrade in arms... precious brother... and wonderful friend... I love walking with you! The MOWTeam that is my family... all with precious names... all with precious purpose... all who are pursuing loving Jesus with low down, laid down love!

Endorsements

I love Danny Steyne's adventurous heart and unwillingness to accept the status quo. I also appreciate that he is a realist who understands that we can and should honor heroes of faith past and present. But their inspiration should lead us to pay our own price. That's what Danny, his family and the MOW team are setting out to do. You will discover the heart of a Jesus revolution in this book. It's a heart that is creative, risky, but somehow humble and bursting with God's love. No book has all the answers. But this one will truly move you to ask the right questions.

Denny Cline

The Albany Vineyard

Albany, Oregon

I have known Danny for more than twenty years and serve along with him on the apostolic team of

Mountain Of Worship. What he writes is not simply what he believes, but what he practices. I recently read his new book "These Walk On Water" during a ministry trip. As I began reading, I was caught up in all the stories that Danny shares and could not put the book down. This book is a call not just to hear words but to bring the reality of experience to a nation. It will challenge and encourage you that truly nothing will be impossible to those that believe.

Jim Reilly

Mountain Of Worship

Columbia, South Carolina

I met a young evangelist on the streets of Los Angeles twenty-five years ago: Danny Steyne. He is more passionate now, but he also is more "Jesus" mature. This book will inspire you to follow Jesus with wisdom and zeal. Danny doesn't trash the present church, but his view of Kingdom life will challenge those who compromise their values. He is concerned with making Kingdom disciples who "are not afraid to follow in the footsteps of those who previously have paid the price." This book relentlessly pulls you from the bleachers onto the playing field.

Bob Fulton

International Coordinator Emeritus

Vineyard Christian Fellowship

Contents

FOREWORD

BY RANDY CLARK

Danny Steyne's new book, *These Walk On Water*, is a "Christian Manifesto" calling for a display of Christianity with power. He writes not as a writer, but as a prophet calling people into their destiny; the destiny of fulfilling the words of Jesus about doing more than he had done because we "believe". This is not the book for the couch potato Christian who has a little cultural religion. Neither is it the book for people who perceive Christianity as "fire insurance". Rather this book is written to call forth those who understand Christianity as a revolutionary call to a new life style; a lifestyle of power to work miracles, heal the sick, cast out demons, minister to the poor, and worship God with abandonment.

These Walk On Water is not a nostalgic book looking back to the "good old days." This is not a backward looking book, but one that looks to the "best of days" in the future great move of God. However, it is not a book about the far off future or the millennium, rather it is a call to prepare now in order to be part of this time of outpouring of miracles, signs and wonders that is already breaking forth. It is a perspective that the Kingdom of God is at hand, it is moving towards the consummation.

Danny's prophetic voice is one of hope to wake up many in the sleeping giant church, awakening them to their potential, to be clothed with power to enable them to express the love and compassion of God, through His power that will work so mightily within them. His voice is a call to faith, not faith as a belief system, but faith as an expectation of God coming and working through the believers, to do through them what He did through Jesus.

I have ministered with Danny and he lives what he writes. He is already seeing God work miracles in his life and ministry. This is not written from a theoretical point of view, but with certainty that the invitation through the spiritual door of opportunity Danny invites us to enter is not only not locked but is standing open. He understands that this is the time of a sovereign invitation into the glory of the latter house which is to be greater than the glory of the former house.

When I read a book I often mark statements that are worthy of notation with N.B., abbreviations for two Latin words which mean "worthy of notation", and I mark Q where there is something I am so impressed with that I think it is worthy of quoting. I found this short book to have many N.B.s and Qs. Time and space won't allow the N.B.s but I want to give you some of the Qs. "Servants beg, friends ask, but sons command." In reference to the generation that is emerging in a miraculous manner he writes, "They are not looking at the past for 'how to's' they are looking to the Father for the 'what now's!" In reference to the voice of Jesus Danny heard in a spiritual dream after seeing the church as a giant body lying in a church building upon waking up stood up and destroyed the structure of the church building he heard Jesus say, "This is what is going to happen when I wake up my church. There is no structure that will be able to contain it!" In a section dealing with hardships to be borne by those co-laboring with Jesus in the supernatural he writes, "This generation that 'walks on water' is a generation that has previously walked through water, through fire, through difficulty . . . through events that baptized them and transformed their very being into something they could not be before." Another Q, "Faithfulness, passion, and fruitfulness is not measured by periods of time, but over the length of a lifetime." Another, "Some have willingly laid down the 'status-quo' church life, in order to experience the 'God invaded life!'" One of my favorite quotes in the book is a longer one, "There never has been a generation that has seen "more than" Jesus saw. This generation is beginning to apprehend it! Heaven is becoming familiar with the faces of this generation as repeatedly they enter the Holy Place and invoke the Presence of God on the earth. This time the story is not about a "theological" answer for men...this time, it's about the raw Love and Power of God demonstrated in ways that will confound the scholar and make believers out of atheists! This generation lives differently, acts differently, sounds differently, and evidently is hearing differently than what its predecessors have heard!"

The sections on worship and its relationship to faith and expectancy are very powerful in their insightfulness to what is needed to have breakthroughs in worship. And the section on converts and discipleship is also very insightful. This section is a must correction to the present mindset within the church. The church isn't called by Jesus to make converts, but disciples. We must not mistake a well-entertained audience for an army. A very important balance in the book is it doesn't only focus on power, but also on love. Danny, like the apostle Paul, doesn't make love the substitute for power or emphasize power working outside the context of love, but like Paul sees the higher way of doing the deeds of the Kingdom of God through the gifts of the Holy Spirit as the way we co-labor with Jesus, and this is done in the love of God the Father. Danny understands that we "labor with all His energy that works so mightily within us" as the Apostle Paul said. He also understands that we are to do this work motivated by His love that also works within us.

I was inspired to press in to become a "water walker", a term Danny uses to describe those who join God in this time which is pregnant with the opportunity to step into a miraculous lifestyle, through the enabling presence of the triune God in our lives.

Would you like to have the opportunity to receive a prophetic word for your life? Would you like to know what God has to say to your life regarding his destiny for you? If so, then read *These Walk On Water* and you will have received a general word from the Lord for your life now.

Randy Clark
Global Awakening Ministries
International Conference Speaker, Author
November 2006

FOREWORD

BY ROLLAND & HEIDI BAKER

Danny Steyne has an appetite for God that will not be denied. Like my wife Heidi and me, his heart is set on seeing what only God can do. He cannot bear the thought of settling for this natural world, and what we can accomplish without the miraculous power of God. He sees what many Christians cannot see, that the Kingdom in all its power is not optional in our lives. We are sustained in every way by His might, and without it we wither away in helplessness and ignorance.

Like Danny, we cannot understand how anyone can be satisfied with testimonies. Instead, the cloud of witnesses that surround us fire us with a holy dissatisfaction with anything less than what has already been experienced by the people of God. We have been shown what is possible in Him, and we are determined not to miss out. Some may be content to live a shadow of what others have experienced, but we are spurred on. We are in a race, and we run to win.

Moderation of our passion for the things of God is not in our "DNA." We have one chance in all of eternity to exercise our faith in our Savior, to demonstrate what we think of our God. This short life on earth is our one window of opportunity to bring eternal glory to God by choosing Him, His ways, and all the glorious benefits of setting Him before us as our God. We resist every effort of our enemy to diminish His place in our hearts, and to devalue what He means in our lives. We appreciate Him and all He can do. We love everything about Him, and everything He does. We anticipate with indescribable expectation all that He will do. We love who He is, and every facet of His personality and abilities. We cannot get enough of Him; we long for more intimacy yet in order to taste all the more the unfathomable depths of what He is able to reveal to us by His power.

Like Peter, we want to jump out of the boat and walk on water with Jesus. The thrill of the miraculous is great only when it is experienced in relationship with Him. We long to do things with Him, to run with Him, to have the power to enjoy life as He enjoys it, to be as unlimited in abundant life as He is. We realize we cannot be His close companion without sharing His outlook and His capacity to do what is pure, excellent and praiseworthy. Some are content to relate to Jesus in a very limited sphere of activity, but His divine power allows our romance with Him to range far and wide, reaching heights of expression made possible only by sharing His nature in every way. In love we become one spirit with Him, and so we must do the works that He did, and even greater works, so that we can remain completely intimate with Him as His life unfolds among us.

We are not after the impersonal. We are not chasing shows of amazing phenomena. We are not seeking fulfillment in gifts and manifestations. He is the prize, the pearl of great price. He is the great lover, and we cannot get too close to Him. We cannot be too emotional over Him. We cannot appreciate Him too much. No, we are extremists! Our hearts are in position to be ravished by everything that He is capable of performing for His own glory. We are safe in Him, knowing that every exertion of His power will only serve to hold us closer to His heart. We enjoy Him; we delight in Him; and in return we receive the desires of our hearts. We refuse nothing; we reject nothing. We are overjoyed by every miraculous act of His, and recognize that under the control of His Spirit every event of our lives is a miracle.

We revel in being His workmanship, and thrive on carrying out the righteous acts that He has prepared since before the foundation of the world. Our joy knows no bounds as we understand that His righteousness includes demonstrating His power in love on behalf of His people. We will not refuse His power. We will not be tepid. We will not be casual. We will not take Him for granted. We set no limits on the joy that we press on to experience. To be alive is to be filled with His power. To enjoy Him requires power. He saves us from our powerlessness and inability to live as He intends.

Danny sets out a vision in this book that lifts our expectations and catalyzes our passion for a miraculous life in Him. It shifts our focus from what we think is acceptable Christian living to what our Creator Himself is looking for from us. He longs for us to make Him our God in our hearts, coming to Him for everything we need for life and godliness. Danny is running the race to win, and in this book he is helping us to run with him. May we drink in and relish every word of this book, a book that our God has miraculously put into our hands.

Rolland and Heidi Baker
IRIS Ministries
Pemba, Mozambique
November 2006

These walk on water...

"The generation that lives
under an open heaven"

CHAPTER ONE

THE ANOINTING THAT COMES

A good friend of mine, an old prophet with years of wounds, adjustments, and ridicule recently shared with me a very interesting story. It had to do with the anointing on his life. He shared about these prophetic Africans called the "River Walkers." It seems that in some odd way one of these profound prophets in Africa imparted a mantle much in the same way that Elisha received a mantle from Elijah. His name was Beggi. He was called a "River Walker," because indeed they had been known to travel across rivers with the word of the Lord.

Others have also experienced this phenomenon. Mel Tari took teams across swollen rivers to reach the unreached in the South Pacific. Didn't Jesus say somewhere that we would do the works that He did?

Our fears of "mystical" experiences such as I shared above prevent us from pressing into the very destiny that God has for us. He has destined us for the nations, and most of us have remained destined for our soft sofa's, in our nice houses, in our nice neighborhoods, with our nice bank accounts, and our safe world.

The choices really are ours. We are people with free wills, and as such we "vote" by our actions, not necessarily by our words. I remember hearing someone say, "You can have respectability or the anointing." Which would you rather have? Paul put it this way. "I'm a fool for Christ!" Whose fool are you?

God is not mocked. But maybe we should be. Maybe his value for anointing eliminates our need for being respectable to the world. Maybe we have "saved" our lives rather than "losing" it. Maybe we should rethink what it is that God desires from our lives, who it is that He longs for us to touch, and how He works through our lives. Maybe, just maybe…

Anointing comes not from proper teaching, effective teaching, or because we lay claim to it. Anointing comes because we have been with "The Anointed One."

I don't pursue the anointing of others. The "heroes" I read about didn't have their own anointing… they carried His! I want His anointing! The double portion…

the one that results in all being healed... the one that touches nations starting with the face in front of me!

It is true that anointing costs. Paul understood that when he pursued not only the "power of His resurrection, but also the fellowship of His sufferings!" Anointing must carry the ability to pursue Him "under circumstances" as well as experience the victory with Him "over circumstances!"

It is this anointing that God is pouring out on the earth. The anointing of Jesus alone will set free captives, overcome sickness, disease, unbelief, and evil in our communities, cities, and nations.

I have chosen to pursue that anointing with all my heart. I know it is caught by being with Him and remains as I remain in Him. It is the evidence of this anointing that so attracts our attention because it doesn't look like a man... it looks like Our King! He is looking for some who will reach a place of divine desperation for His Presence... for some who will throw the other leg out of the boat and walk on water!

CHAPTER TWO

THE STIRRING OF FAITH

*T*here is something stirring in the earth. There is a movement that is predicated on nothing but passionate hearts for God who have a profound frustration at church as they know it. Their exasperation is producing an extraordinary return to the parameters of Biblical Christianity that have long since been ignored, explained away, or forgotten by a significant portion of the church. These are the days of unprecedented breakthrough when nations will be saved in a "day". These are the days when "wise and persuasive words" will be replaced with a "demonstration of the Spirit and power!"[1]

One young man whom God uses significantly recently shared that in visiting the world of Islam he makes the bold, in fact audacious, statement that if these Muslims can produce someone whom Jesus doesn't heal through him, they can consider him a false prophet! Repeatedly, he has witnessed Jesus touch life after life with the incredible healing power of Jesus, and Muslims are turning to the Lord in droves! Recently, during a campaign in Asia over a quarter of a million responded to the demonstrated message of Jesus through this man and were powerfully saved!

Where is the Lord God of Elijah? Maybe we should ask, "Where is the Lord God of us?" Why have we been afraid to follow in the footsteps of those who have previously paid the price? Why do we stop well before the Jordan? Why do we fail to go through it into the place where our predicament requires miraculous intervention? Why do we remain in Gilgal; the place where our reproach was rolled away and we enjoy salvation but never pursue the higher destiny of His Vision? Why is that we so easily stop at a Bethel; the place of visitation where visions and dreams are enough to carry us? Why is it that we are satisfied with Jericho where once the miracles happened, where once the walls were destroyed? How can we find peace in our memories that it is good enough that God did it once? Where we can revel in the fact of past, historical, factual, miracles, but are so unlike that first generation of promise takers that would walk across a Jordan and back in and out in the midst of miracles occurring in their lives?

The interest of heaven is so different from the interests of men. Scripture records a single question that will be asked at the conclusion of this era of human history. "When the Son of Man comes, will he find faith on the earth?" The issue is not, nor has ever been, how much have we accomplished that we believe is important. The measuring stick is not numbers, not kingdoms, not popularity. The value of heaven is faith. One quick read of the heroes of faith[3] reveals that the treasures of God's heart were those whose lives were measured by faith.

Why is that so few will look past the man who has been used by God, to the God who used a man? Why is it that we have fallen prey to the idolatry of a Christianity that is powerless? Where are those who will say "I'm going across. I'm going out, to come back in. This time when I enter the promises, I'm entering with His Power and His Authority. This time I am going to apprehend His Favor and His Blessing by radical extreme faith! No longer will I be satisfied with the stories of others. I will have my own stories, for I too am a child of the Living God!"

There is a generation that is waking up to the power of God. They will never be consoled with what once was. They will only be satisfied with Him, His Presence, and His Power that is real, authentic, genuine, and exciting!

As I set out to write this book, it is with the hope that I can somehow reach through the pages into your life and pull you into the hope that you have of God's purposes in your life. Some reading this book have given up on those promises long ago. Others of you have wandered long and hard along the banks of His promises for you. You can see the Harvest on the other side. You can almost taste it! You have had prophetic words. You probably have had dreams and visions yourself, but are holding out for something magical to open up the river. It is my hope that I can pull you into this river and watch your joy as you walk across to the waiting fulfillment of God's destiny for you.

I have heard for years that the church is to be prophetic. I know that statement is true, but it is also inadequate. There is something beyond the prophetic. Some might call it apostolic, but whatever it is called, it results in you walking in the fulfillment of your destiny.

Titles never have mattered much to me. I don't care what you call yourself. It doesn't matter at all if you have title, position, or none at all. I just know that Jesus wants you "pulled" into your destiny. He wants you to experience the fulfillment of your destiny, not simply have it prophesied to you. It is His purpose for you that everything He has destined you for will be completed with incredible value, success, and joy! That is my heart for this book.

Three distinct reactions occur when a crisis or significant need opposes our destiny. There will be those who see the event as obstacles that now hinder our purpose and we plead with God for it's removal. Others will see the event as something that we need to pray through until God somehow removes it so we can accomplish our destiny. But few see it as an opportunity to release the mustard seed faith with authority. This last response results in fulfillment, the others merely look spiritual.

Servants beg, friends ask, but sons command. Only those who have experienced the love of Father God can really release the purpose of His Heart, because they have leaned against His Heart and no great faith is required. Faith, healing, and miracles are not profound events in heaven. The Father always does those things... it is His nature. When we have relationship as a son with Him... we enter into that place of destiny on His lap, hearing Him speak, and authority to speak to crisis and event becomes ours.

I really do believe that God, and all of creation, is waiting for a generation that will "get it!" A generation that not only proclaims, but releases the Gospel with power. A generation that is comfortable with His realm more than their own.

Sons have authority and "right" to command mountains and walk on water if the purposes of God lay ahead of them. Mountains must move to accommodate God's purposes. Water must support the weightiness of His Plans!

If you feel your heart being pulled towards your destiny as you read this book, go with it. Don't resist the Holy Spirit's prompting. You just might find yourself walking on water!

1. 1 Corinthians 4:2
2. Luke 18:8
3. Hebrews 11

CHAPTER THREE

THESE WALK ON WATER

This is what the LORD says to you: 'Do not be afraid or discouraged because of this vast army. For the battle is not yours, but God's. Tomorrow march down against them. You will not have to fight this battle. Take up your positions; stand firm and see the deliverance the LORD will give you. Do not be afraid; do not be discouraged. Go out to face them tomorrow, and the LORD will be with you.'" As they set out, Jehoshaphat stood and said, "Listen to me, Judah and people of Jerusalem! Have faith in the LORD your God and you will be upheld; have faith in his prophets and you will be successful." Jehoshaphat appointed men to sing to the LORD and to praise him for the splendor of his holiness as they went out at the head of the army, saying: "Give thanks to the LORD, for his love endures forever." As they began to sing and praise, the LORD set ambushes against the men of Ammon and Moab and Mount Seir who were invading Judah, and they were defeated.

2 Chronicles 20:15-17, 20-22

"Lord, did I really hear you right; are you really asking me to simply step out in faith? Isn't that being irresponsible? Isn't that being presumptuous?"

I had planted a church in North Carolina; we had some significant times with the Lord there. Karen and I had walked a traditional church through an inevitable transition prior to the planting, and we saw the Lord do some incredible things through the church we helped birth.

One period of ten months saw people coming from across the nation, and even from overseas, but at the end of that ten-month event of almost nightly meetings, we realized there was so much more available from God than what we had experienced. There was also so much more of what we wanted to experience. We became desperate for it! We knew that church as we had known it was about to change. We began a journey hoping to see a church that would be filled with the Power of God and rife with His Presence!

There were a few people whom God used to radically turn our world upside down. One couple from Mozambique had a major influence on our desperation.

Each time we saw Rolland and Heidi Baker, we were astounded by the fact that God was using these two precious servants in such a profound way. We personally longed to see such a release in our own lives as well.

We heard stories that, had they not been verifiable, could be considered legends. But they were verifiable. The stories were true. They were the Book of Acts now!

The dead were being raised, the blind were seeing, the lame were walking, food was being multiplied so many times that they had lost count! In the first few years of their ministry in Mozambique, the Bakers saw a small church and about three hundred orphans impacted by the Gospel through their lives. In the next seven years they would see over seven thousand churches planted, thousands of orphans embraced into their lives, and over a million people touched through their ministry in Africa!

The most incredible thing about the Bakers was that they were simply in love with Jesus. The powerful impact of love flowing through them touched so many. I can assure you, it was their love that touched Karen and I and drove us past the servants to the One who holds that Love, and for that we are so grateful that God allowed us to cross the path of the Bakers.

Another young man, with a ruthless love for Jesus, regularly witnesses multitudes touched by the power of God and healed from every manner of disease! We heard stories of millions saved in China, hundreds of thousands of Muslims coming to Jesus in Africa and the Middle East.

We heard stories of the dead being raised and the blind seeing! Our hearts became drawn towards the lifestyle of the Book of Acts. We wanted that with all our hearts!

Karen and I realized something profound was taking place around the earth, and we did not want to miss any of it. More than that, we believed that if this same Jesus could touch others in other third world nations, then His Power was also available to be released to this nation and other first world nations with that same manifest healing power!

We were ruined. It was a positive effect, but nevertheless, we could no longer function as we had in the past. Pastoring and planting churches was no longer the dream it had once been. We now wanted to see fulfilled the dramatic promises of God that set men free and healed blind men and women. We now didn't simply want to hear the stories of how God did it somewhere, we wanted to see the stories happening through our own lives, and through the lives of those we touched. We were ready to do anything in order to see this happen.

That is when I was given a very unique commission by the Lord.

One Sunday night I was leading a "Night of Worship" in a large church in South Carolina. As I sang I began seeing a vision of a mountain emerging from the flat ground. Eventually the mountain was larger than anything around it, and in fact everything around it bore its shadow. Very quickly, it became volcanic and released "worship" in the form of volcanic ash and debris all over the region, all over the nation, and throughout the nations. It was a vision I had seen about fifteen years previously, expecting to see the fulfillment of it then. The difference this time was that I heard the voice of the Father say, "You haven't seen this yet, but you are about to!" I knew that I was about to embark on a journey into a dramatic alteration of lifestyle and a new path lay before me.

I knew that this commission was different from any other role I had played in the church. It was both exciting and frightening at the same time. It would require instant, immediate obedience, and the first step would be to step into the water, not knowing what was there. I knew I had to return to Columbia, South Carolina as a part of the first step in this process of obedience.

Within a few days, my wife and I realized the profound and wonderful purpose of God that was correcting and adjusting us beyond the point of the comfortable, familiar, and safe, but we were excited. We knew that God was leading us into the destiny of our lives! We packed, gave away, sold off, and got ready for something new. What it looked like, I had no idea, but I knew Someone who did know, and that was enough! Six weeks later, we relocated to Columbia, to see a volcanic eruption of worship. We would have to wait for several months before we saw steam break through the surface and that would only be the start!

For Karen and I, we decided that no longer did we want to stand on the banks and watch. No longer did we want to peer into the "promised land" with the hopes of something magical that would bring us from where we were, to where we wanted to be. No longer did we want to see others go across without going there ourselves. No longer did we aspire to be historians and reporters of what God once did, we wanted to live in it. We were ready to pay the price. We were ready to become two of those who "walk on water!"

The cost was immediate. We had to step out on "faith without hints." God was the only One allowed to know our needs... not His people. We left income and found Him faithful to provide, supernaturally, as He always has for His servants. He indicated clearly it was time for generation to know who Jehovah Jireh was. Not simply a "provider," but rather the Lord "who sees to it!" The Lord who "pays for what He orders!" We very quickly realized the stability of this water we were walking on. It was His environment, and as such, much more conducive to Him fulfilling His purposes through our lives!

We fumbled into the process of walking with Him. We weren't used to it. We had always had the security of a ministry position that paid. This was very different. I wasn't even sure what God was calling me to do. Everything was different. My paradigm had changed.

For two years we met with about a dozen of us in our home. We weren't even sure what we were doing with that. All we knew is that we had to figure out how to really love each other and then release His love everywhere we went. We chose restaurants as our venue to release His love and went out to eat often, always releasing Kingdom to the waiter or waitress, and often to the cook or people at nearby tables. We often watched as God touched people and literally as they wept and fell to their knees in response.

Nothing we were doing was remotely like church we had done. When we gathered it was to simply be family together. Sometimes it included worship or a study, but more often than not it was simply developing this wonderful relationship with each other and Jesus. Nothing looked like a meeting anymore. I loved it more than I had anything in my previous Christian walk... and that was more than forty years at that time! It finally felt like maybe we were glimpsing at the doorway of what Jesus meant when He said "My Church!"

We never felt like we had to hold on to anybody. These were Jesus' sheep, not ours. We never had to try and replicate something great we had seen in a conference or another church. We just simply needed to listen to Him.

It is a walk of faith. Ongoing faith. Never ending faith. Eternal faith. God began teaching us that "faith," just like love and hope, will continue to be in eternity, because faith IS the realm of God. He lives in it. Creation was brought forth in faith before men existed. The New Heavens and New Earth will be released through the faith of God.

When we begin to operate in faith... not mustered faith, but mustard seed faith... we enter the realm of God. It is the place of Jubilee. It is the place of Destiny now. It is the place of "on earth as it is in heaven!" It is in fact the place where we can walk on water towards the destination of our beloved King!

CHAPTER FOUR

THE JOSEPH GENERATION

he blind receive sight, the lame walk, those who have leprosy are cured, the deaf hear, the dead are raised, and the good news is preached to the poor... I tell you the truth, anyone who has faith in me will do what I have been doing. He will do even greater things than these, because I am going to the Father.

Matthew 11:5, John 14:12

Open your eyes. Open your ears. Have you heard the stories? Have you seen the reports? Has your heart jumped with excitement as you realize that God is moving extraordinarily throughout the earth beyond anything you could have ever imagined?

One significant, repeated occurrence that is taking place throughout the world is unprecedented in history. The dead are being raised in more frequency than ever. In fact, it seems that with believers in the Western World, there is a pre- occupation with "resurrection power". Believers everywhere are now declaring that this kind of demonstration must now be released in the Western World in fulfillment of the promises of Jesus to do the "greater works".

Something else has also been happening, supernaturally, and beyond the norm. Many believers have been gathering in homes, churches, communities, and conferences spanning the denominational and non-denominational churches without desire for specific recognition.

Titles are giving way to function. After all the hoopla of the past several years of the release of the "five-fold" ministry we may be learning our lessons. What most are finding out is that it's not about "five-fold" ministry; it's about the "sheep-fold" ministry of Jesus!

No one knows more the value of the prophetic or apostolic calling in people's lives; I've experienced the blessing of it in my life. But it's not the title on a person that produces fruit, it's the function of that calling through their life. Most often, I have found that the more individuals hold on to a title, the less effective they are; whereas the more they give place to simply functioning in their calling, the greater fruitfulness emerges.

When the sheep become acquainted with the Shepherd, valuable, fruitful ministry will emerge. That is the first mark of this generation. As one seasoned prophetic voice called it years ago, "it's a faceless generation... a new breed of servants!"

How this generation is emerging is nothing short of miraculous. They are not looking at the past for "how to's" they are looking to the Father for the "what now's!" I call it the "favored son" and right now, that son is being revealed. Some have called it the Tribe of Joseph, but whatever you call it; it is beginning to stand up!

Ȕ&#x16;2&#x16;H

Now Israel loved Joseph more than any of his other sons, because he had been born to him in his old age; and he made a richly ornamented robe for him. When his brothers saw that their father loved him more than he loved any of them, they hated him and could not speak a kind word to him.

Genesis 37:3-4

Jacob loved Joseph more than he loved any of his other sons and because of this favoritism", he was given a robe of many colors. Most of us have read the story, but there is far more to the story than a simple reading of it. That robe was far more than just a multi-colored robe, it represented far more than favoritism; it represented Joseph's authority over each of his brothers.

During the era of Jacob and Joseph, much like various tribes throughout the world today, each tribe had a specific color that represented their lineage and heritage. That specific color identified them and their uniqueness. Joseph's robe included many colors. It is easy to surmise that many, if not all, of the colors that represented each of their unique families were included in his robe. Jacob was in fact declaring prophetically that Joseph had authority beyond the parameters of his own tribe, into the tribes even of his own brothers.

Through the dramatic event of the colored cloak, Joseph's father unwittingly declared prophetically that Joseph's dreams of having authority over his family would one day come about. Joseph was uniquely set apart from his brethren. The calling on Joseph's life was set up not only to a divine purpose, but also to a divine mandate of difficulty that would facilitate the making of a man of character. Although Jacob never considered the ramifications of the cloak and hatred that ensued, The Father knew that these events would result in Joseph's ability to handle the anointing and authority that would come later in His life.

Joseph's life was full of great difficulty, but he never wavered from his purpose, and his heart remained free from bitterness. The hardship and choices of character and integrity that he was faced with brought him repeatedly to the place where only God could vindicate. I am sure that God's timetable was often much longer than Joseph's, but he allowed no acrimony in his life.

The sign of a Joseph Generation is that they will not allow pain and hardship in anyway to taint their love for God and his purposes for them in the earth. They truly will become "better" not "bitter". Joseph demonstrated that hardship could not deter him from apprehending the promises of God, so long as his heart remained pure and faithful in every circumstance.

After the restoration of Joseph to Israel and his family, favor pours over the entire family. Joseph's willingness to endure persecution and hardship and even the loss of his family was the groundwork that set the stage for multiplied favor. Far beyond a simple colored cloak, he now received a double portion of blessing that came back to his family. When Jesus indicates that we bless those who curse us, it is with the intent that one day they will experience the blessing on our lives. His heart is always to bless!

The blessing given by fathers during that period of history gives clarity to the enormous favor he experienced. Israel's blessing of Joseph far outweighed all the other blessings that were apportioned to the tribes of Israel. To each of Israel's sons there were future hopes, but the blessings to Joseph exceeded all of his brothers.

"Joseph is a fruitful vine, a fruitful vine near a spring, whose branches climb over a wall. With bitterness, archers attacked him; they shot at him with hostility. But his bow remained steady. His strong arms stayed limber, because of the hand of the Mighty One of Jacob, because of the Shepherd, the Rock of Israel, because of your father's God, who helps you, because of the Almighty, who blesses you with blessings of the heavens above, blessings of the

deep that lies below, blessings of the breast and womb. Your father's blessings are greater than the blessings of the ancient mountains, than the bounty of the age-old hills. Let all these rest on the head of Joseph, on the brow of the prince among his brothers."

Genesis 49:22-26

However, not only did Joseph receive a blessing, his sons also received a blessing from Israel, something that none of the other brothers received. Truly, his blessing was the greatest!

Years pass. About four hundred years later, God instructed the people of Israel to leave Egypt. By this time, the "Tribe of Joseph" ceased to exist under his name. The tribes of Manasseh and Ephraim rise up as mighty tribes of the sons of Joseph, and displace the tribe of Joseph two-fold, double portion, double anointing!

The allotted portions in the Promised Land for each of the tribes of Joseph are as significant individually, as any of the other tribes. But the favor does not stop at the double anointing. When the tribes of Manasseh and Ephraim ask Joshua for more, he gives it to them. Their authority extended with boldness into abundance, not simply need.

Favor surrounded the lives of Joseph and his sons, but it was the early years, the years of Joseph's suffering, that seemed to be the years where there was no favor and where Joseph paid the price for the favor that would one day be released.

Today there is a generation rising. A generation that has walked through the pain and difficulty of carrying promises without evidence of fulfillment anywhere in sight. Repeatedly they have been called upon to serve and they have served well. Yet so often seems it has appeared that just when they were about to reach the point where destiny was going to be fulfilled, they were brought back to places of obscurity and hardship and their message has been forgotten.

That is where Joseph's are made! In obscurity, in exile, in pits and prisons! And this tribe of Joseph must now arise! Having paid the price, now this tribe will begin revealing the purposes and wisdom of God throughout the nations!

Who is this tribe? It is all of those that journey through times of hardship with joy. This tribe is all of those who embrace that difficulty without bitterness. It is you, if you welcome those difficulties that come your way as God's plan for bringing you into the place of God! It is you, who will reach the place of promise and destiny and become a part of the "Tribe of Joseph"!

CHAPTER FIVE

THE ANOINTING IS IN THE BONES

ow they buried the bones of Joseph, which the sons of Israel brought up from Egypt, at Shechem, in the piece of ground which Jacob had bought from the sons of Hamor the father of Shechem for one hundred pieces of money; and they became the inheritance of Joseph's sons.

Joshua 24:32

The anointing of Joseph doesn't end with his death. It doesn't end with the blessing of his sons. It doesn't even end with the inheritance they received in the Promised Land. The anointing continued with his bones!

Prior to his death, Joseph asked that his bones be carried back to the land of Promise. His request was more than simply a nice burial gesture, Joseph understood destiny. He had experienced it fully, and he knew that the ultimate destiny for all of God's people is to be living in the promises given. God's purposes for Joseph were not complete at his death, they would continue in the burial of his bones. This is not some superstitious response that Joseph had in requesting that his bones be buried in the Promised Land. Joseph had a comprehension of the Ways of God that we often miss.

The Bible speaks of bones in a unique way.

ഐരു

"Once while some Israelites were burying a man, suddenly they saw a band of raiders; so they threw the man's body into Elisha's tomb. When the body touched Elisha's bones, the man came to life and stood up on his feet."

2 Kings 13:21

Elisha's bones carried very real power. This was no magical or superstitious event. This very real experience resulted in the resurrection of a man. Elisha was dead, but evidently, his anointing never died!

Could Elisha have been one of the Holy Men who was raised during the resurrection?[1] Only eternity will tell, but clearly, there was something of God's resurrection power that rested on more than only Elisha's bones. God's preoccupation of evidencing life on what was once dead is not only a historical fact, but reveals something of the character of God!

Paul's preoccupation with God's power over death inspires this generation! "Where, O death, is your victory? Where, O death, is your sting?" is reminiscent of someone like Elisha who would cry, "Where is the Lord God of Elijah?" Both reflect that the evidence of God releases the miraculous Power of God.

The generation that sees the power of God is a generation who understands the attributes of God! For them, there is no audacity to demanding "heaven on earth," they understand the authority which has been given to them.

When the rest of the world sees death and bones, this generation sees a God who is aroused to move by such a sight!

Joseph evidently had a revelatory understanding of the purposes of God, not only for his life, but also for the generations that would follow. He also understood that anointing of God's wisdom and power rested on his life, and it was intended for his seed.

He had no ability other than that which God gave him. Moreover, all the hardship and difficulty he endured had allowed for a measure of God in his life that he wanted to leave as an inheritance for his people. Joseph wanted the anointing of His life (the favor, wisdom and wealth of God) to be carried with the people of Israel to the Land of Promise. Interestingly enough, today much of the world's wealth is held by the Jewish people who have been given a precision wisdom, much like Joseph. Could it be that the anointing followed him?

The ancients believed that "power" and "anointing" rested in the bones. Enemies would burn, crush & break bones of their adversaries in order to prevent "power" and "anointing" from continuing on beyond the life of their enemy. For millennia this behavior continued. A pivotal part of conquering an enemy was the desecration of their bones.

The bones of the righteous were to be buried with respect and dignity. The bones of the wicked were to be burned, crushed, given to dogs, and eradicated from the earth.

Jezebel's bones were all eaten by dogs; a testimony to the fact that God had no intention of her evil ways being ever replicated again. [3] Those who accused Daniel were thrown to the lions and their "bones were all crushed", another testimony that God had no intention of allowing the spirit of accusation on them to be released on anyone else! [4]

The bones held life in them. The marrow in them, can affect the disposition of a persons health and future. When Jeremiah cries out that the message of God is within his bones, he gives us imagery of God's purposes exuding from his bones. [5] And then there is David.

ဆာ

Cleanse me with hyssop, and I will be clean; wash me, and I will be whiter than snow. Let me hear joy and gladness; let the bones you have crushed rejoice. Hide your face from my sins and blot out all my iniquity. Create in me a pure heart, O God, and renew a steadfast spirit within me. Do not cast me from your presence or take your Holy Spirit from me. Restore to me the joy of your salvation and grant me a willing spirit, to sustain me.

Psalm 51:7-12

After David's murderous affair with Bathsheba, He finds himself crying out to God for "bones" that rejoice. In this particular narrative, God crushes David's bones. David's obvious sin opened the door for the "crushing" that would "drain off" anointing. Later David cries, *"Do not cast me from your presence or take your Holy Spirit from me."* The cry was a very real predicament that David was experiencing. He was experiencing a distance from God and a pulling back of God's Holy Spirit from his life. The anointing was lifting.

His cry was for a restoration of the bones that were crushed. His cry was that God would restore the anointing, the power, and the sense of God's overwhelming Grace on His life!

The holy generation that is emerging, is emerging out of dry bones. The anointing is good. The power to overcome is about to be released onto them... and then through them as this mighty vast army of bones arises and releases the authority and power and anointing of God on this earth!

1. The tombs broke open and the bodies of many holy people who had died

were raised to life. 53 They came out of the tombs, and after Jesus' resurrection they went into the holy city and appeared to many people. (Matthew 27:52-53)

2. 1 Corinthians 15:55

3. But when they went out to bury her, they found nothing except her skull, her feet and her hands. *(36)* They went back and told Jehu, who said, "This is the word of the LORD that he spoke through his servant Elijah the Tishbite: On the plot of ground at Jezreel dogs will devour Jezebel's flesh. *(37)* Jezebel's body will be like refuse on the ground in the plot at Jezreel, so that no one will be able to say, 'This is Jezebel.'" (2 Kings9:35-37 NIV)

4. At the king's command, the men who had falsely accused Daniel were brought in and thrown into the lions' den, along with their wives and children. And before they reached the floor of the den, the lions overpowered them and crushed all their bones. (Daniel 6:24 NIV)

5. But if I say, "I will not mention him or speak any more in his name," his word is in my heart like a fire, a fire shut up in my bones. I am weary of holding it in; indeed, I cannot. (Jeremiah 20:9)

CHAPTER SIX

THE VALLEY OF DRY BONES

*T*he hand of the LORD was upon me, and he brought me out by the Spirit of the LORD and set me in the middle of a valley; it was full of bones. He led me back and forth among them, and I saw a great many bones on the floor of the valley, bones that were very dry. He asked me, "Son of man, can these bones live?" I said, "O Sovereign LORD, you alone know." Then he said to me, "Prophesy to these bones and say to them, 'Dry bones, hear the word of the LORD! This is what the Sovereign LORD says to these bones: I will make breath enter you, and you will come to life. I will attach tendons to you and make flesh come upon you and cover you with skin; I will put breath in you, and you will come to life. Then you will know that I am the LORD.'" So I prophesied as I was commanded. And as I was prophesying, there was *a noise, a rattling sound, and the bones came together, bone to bone. I looked, and tendons and flesh appeared on them and skin covered them, but there was no breath in them. Then he said to me, "Prophesy to the breath; prophesy, son of man, and say to it, 'This is what the Sovereign LORD says: Come from the four winds, O breath, and breathe into these slain, that they may live.'" So I prophesied as he commanded me, and breath entered them; they came to life and stood up on their feet—a vast army. Then he said to me: "Son of man, these bones are the whole house of my people. They say, 'Our bones are dried up and our hope is gone; we are cut off.' Therefore prophesy and say to them: 'This is what the Sovereign LORD says: O my people, I am going to open your graves and bring you up from them; I will bring you back to the land of your destiny. Then you, my people, will know that I am the LORD, when I open your graves and bring you up from them. I will put my Spirit in you and you will live, and I will settle you in your own land. Then you will know that I the LORD have spoken, and I have done it, declares the LORD.'"*

Ezekiel 37:1-14

Generations pass. The bones of Joseph are there. The bones of the righteous are there. The bones of those who have carried the heart after God, with no bitterness, are there. Those bones with generations of powerful anointing lay before the prophet Ezekiel. All of the bones are dry; all of them are apparently laying in unorganized piles throughout a vast valley, without any sense of life in them.

Before this event, the bones simply were there. After this event, the nations would tremble and army of the Lord would go forth with might and power.

The nation is in a shambles, is there hope anymore? He looks at the bones scattered before him, the desire is for that anointing to once again fill the earth. He looks at the lack of life lying before him. The mess. The history that was. The lives that were. From here he realizes that his generation, and the generations to come are completely bankrupt without the mantles of these Abraham's, Joseph's, Deborah's, Miriam's, Joshua's, Elisha's, David's, and Samuel's who moved with such authority that heaven aligned with destinies of these men and women!

The Spirit whispers, "prophesy son of man, prophesy!" His heart hears the provocation of heaven, "don't you want to see My Power released in greater ways than you have ever seen?" "Prophesy, son of man, prophesy!" Ezekiel's heart cries for that kind of release. Oh, God do you really want me to do that? The goading continues, "Prophesy, son of man, prophesy!"

"Do you think they can live Ezekiel?" The incitement of God burns in his heart! "God, you alone know if they can live!" The reply blasts back "Oh, no Ezekiel, I'm not letting you off that easy! Prophesy, son of man, prophesy!"

The prophets' heart melts. How can I a little man, just one set of living bones, prophesy to so many dead, lifeless bones? How can I release authority to those generations prior to mine and say live? I'm not as good as the

Abraham's, Joseph's, Deborah's, Miriam's, Joshua's, Elisha's, David's, Samuel's ... I'm simply a little prophet born to prophesy a small word 600 years prior to the Messiah. I'm the prophet who does strange things and no one takes me seriously. How can I prophesy to these bones?

The reply comes back with the full weight of heaven "Because I said so Ezekiel... Prophesy, son of man, prophesy!"

And so Ezekiel fumbles for words he never has spoken before. He looks at the dry bones... and raises his voice. "Live!"

The bones come together, the sinews and muscles and flesh form around the bones, but resurrection power has not yet happened. Great miracle Ezekiel... but it's not enough... you have to press all the way into the fulfillment of this prophesy... you have to pull this generation onto it's feet!

Heaven goads some more! "Prophesy to the breath!!!! Let resurrection power come!" Ezekiel prompted by the apparent miracle happening before him raises his voice with more boldness... "Breathe! Rise up Oh Army of God!"

And as he did, the vast army arose. The Army of Joel 2, the Army of the Lord. The Tribe of Joseph. The generation of Resurrection Power. The mantles were restored... the anointing was about to be released!

We have heard of the "wells that God is redigging" throughout this nation and around the world. Many have been seeking out the mantles of those forerunners who ran with such passion and power. It appears as if the mantles have been recovered, and most of the church believes that is sufficient. But the anointing, the breath, must come from God alone.

Mantles are merely realms of authority. They lack power. Power comes from God alone. Anointing comes from those who get to God on their own, not through someone who simply has grabbed a mantle.

Scripture is clear on this matter. How many kings held mantles, without the anointing of their fathers? Elisha's anointing was very different from Elijah's, but his sphere of authority was the same. It was to the entire region of Israel.

The breath must come on the bones before we can effectively touch this world… we must be touched by God alone, not grandfathered in by our inheritance or those who have gone on before. We must seek Him for that which comes from Him. I don't really want a man's anointing. I want the anointing that flows out of The Anointed One… Jesus!

The wicked are in great dread, For God is with the righteous generation.

Psalm 14:5

Something is happening, and it eclipses anything we have seen previously. We are beginning to witness a generation that is striking fear in places of darkness. We are beginning to see death displaced by life and evil displaced by righteousness.

We are living in a time where BREATH is being poured out, RESSURECTION POWER. The BREATH OF GOD!

God has been pulling things together prophetically for generations, but now the four winds are beginning to blow by the Spirit on the corpse that surrounds the anointing, the anointing of the ages. The tribe of Joseph is about to rise.

This generation is the Joseph Generation. The Anointed Generation. This Tribe of Joseph wears the colors of many tribes, and many nations. It has the opportunity to be distinct from previous generations as long as they do not become exclusive to one denomination, movement, or group.... This generation spans the globe. But its greatest distinction is the love, the power and the anointing that flows through it.

The White Country Church

In 1982 I was ministering to gangs in Southern California... at least I thought I was. I was going out daily, witnessing daily, sharing daily.... But saw very little power!

In November 1982 I had a dream. This dream was unlike any I had ever had. I knew the dream was a message from God to me, and I knew it would mark my life permanently.

In the dream I saw a little white country church, the kind you see on calendars. It was very scenic and picturesque. I went inside the church and could see laying across the pews, from front to back, a huge giant that lay asleep, face down, with his head near the pulpit and his feet near the entrance.

Without warning, a large hand broke through the ceiling and reached down to the shoulder of the giant. The hand then shook the giant awake. Immediately the giant pushed up and then stood up tall. The structure of the building was not built to withstand the size or power of that giant, and it absolutely was decimated. It looked much like a mobile home after a tornado gets through with it, everything was strewn everywhere and every part was splintered and broken.

I then heard these words. "This is what is going to happen when I wake up my church. There is no structure that will be able to contain it!"

That dream affected me for many years, always looking for the giant to stand up. A few years ago I lived across the street from a church that looked just like the one in my dream... in fact I pastored it.... But the hope was not in that church... the hope was in the giant that would rise from it! I believe he is pushing through the rafters right now!

"The girl is not dead but asleep." But they laughed at him.

Matthew 9:24

After he had said this, he went on to tell them, "Our friend Lazarus has fallen asleep; but I am going there to wake him up."

John 11:11

"Wake up, O sleeper, rise from the dead, and Christ will shine on you."

Ephesians 5:14

Jesus often used the term asleep when actually someone was dead!

These days, right now, are the days where God is awakening a generation with the Breath of Life, it is time to prophesy to the corpse, live, breathe, resurrect…. wake up!

This Tribe of Joseph will arise, not in division, but in unity; not in category, but in power; not as a movement, but as a bride…. spanning the globe with a demonstration of His Love, His Power and His Authority and it will elude definition and denominationalism…. It truly will bear the Marks of Him!

"So I prophesied as he commanded me, and breath entered them; they came to life and stood up on their feet—a vast army."

Ezekiel 37:9-10

CHAPTER SEVEN

SUCK IT UP AND LOVE IT!

$\mathcal{A}$nd so we continue this journey after those who will walk on water. Do we really want it that bad?

We have heard their stories. I most certainly have. The stories about those who are beginning to experience "the stuff." [1] Some believe it's shameful to share the stories, that we must hide those things out of humility. It stirs up a jealousy in us when we hear that the dead are being raised, the blind receiving sight, the lame walking. We don't realize it's a holy jealousy to provoke us to love and good deeds. Without that jealousy we would never press in to the cost.

How many of us know that there really is a cost! Jesus indicated cost! All the disciples endured great cost!

Throughout the centuries those who have experienced the powerful moves of God have all endured great cost! Guess what? If we are going to experience the fullness of His Power... we will also experience some of the cost as well.

A couple years ago while traveling through Atlanta I was sharing my delight of recent meetings I had been in with a Christian Leader who works with the poor. The meetings had been incredible. The couple that I was rejoicing about had been experiencing power of Biblical proportions with healings and miracles and even the dead being raised. I was ecstatic. My friend, a mature brother, responded with a question that rang in my spirit for weeks. "That's great you want to see that, but are you really willing to pay the price? Do you know all they went through to experience what they are experiencing now?"

I didn't consider cost. But began to realize that "cost" was critical to "clout" in the Kingdom! The heavier the cost, the greater the authority!

I now understand something for the church! I have a very clear, very specific word! It's time... it's time... it's time!!!! It's time to get over it! It's time to suck it up and embrace it! The cost often will first come to us in regard to personal hurt and wounding, that God is wanting us to embrace not cry over.

If you have been hurt, offended, broken or in any way feel burned out.... it is TIME to embrace your burn out and the places that God took you for that to occur! It wasn't to destroy you, it was to build you!

Those who walk on water get wounded daily, but never consider the wounds as great as the joy of living in His Love! We must constantly embrace the insecurity of trusting again and again, and reach out again and again, and allowing our vision to be worn on our sleeve again!

Isn't that what all of the ancients endured? Isn't that what Jesus Himself endured? Have all our inventions and modernizations and attitudes towards life removed the basic premise of our Christian Faith.... "no servant is above His Master?" [2]

Then Jesus was led by the Spirit into the desert to be tempted by the devil.

Matthew 4:1

It is the nature of our walk with God that adversity will occur. It is adversity and difficulty that mature and grow us up in Him. It was the adversity of the desert that God led His people through for forty years, hoping, waiting for them to not be complainers and whiners. It was their greatest hour to demonstrate faithfulness and admiration of a God who would take care of their every need.

When Jesus was led "by the Spirit" into the desert, he didn't run from it, he embraced it. Every battle and affliction of the desert, He knew, were to produce the character needed of any servant of God, and the ramifications of anointing are in direct proportion to our willingness to embrace hardship and difficulty.

Much of the teaching out there tries to remove believers from places of growth and maturity. We have emphasized comfort above character! The result has left us in a crisis. The truth of maturity in leadership has been replaced by a doctrine that has taught that if you are walking with God it is a life of ease... and so we have modified the Gospel that speaks of integrity and character with a message of "comfort me.... I don't deserve to hurt... I don't believe I should be bleeding!"

But where do we get the marks for ourselves? Where do we get the wounds that reflect His character?

Finally, let no one cause me trouble, for I bear on my body the marks of Jesus.

Galatians 6:17

Now I rejoice in what was suffered for you, and I fill up in my flesh what is still lacking in regard to Christ's afflictions, for the sake of his body, which is the church.

Colossians 1:24

The Word is full of this message of suffering and difficulty. Never is it simply something to get along without, in fact it appears than while it is not to be sought, when it arrives, the purpose is God's promotion for our lives to make us more like Jesus. [3]

How can you suck it up? How can you simply "move on?"

No one, including myself, was saying it didn't hurt! If there is one thing apparent to those of us in the Kingdom who have called themselves "family" with each other, it's that we have all been through difficulty in the past and as a result were experience scattering, pain, embarrassment, shame, and in many cases blame!

When I walked through my time of "restoration" [4] ...many of those who were near me went through the difficulty and pain of watching someone they loved being wounded and as a result... many of those were scattered all over the place. Emotions went wild, reactions were vehement, the pain was beyond all of our "pain" threshold. (To this day there are still those who oppose me and directly contribute to an ongoing process where I must constantly forgive and release. The wounds continue, but the joy is worth it!)

What happened to me after I walked through that difficulty was the likely effect of the false teaching that "bad things don't happen to good people!" So many of us have endured this kind of difficulty without appropriate teaching and help that it has created a crisis in the Body of Christ where suffering is never to play any part of our lives!

We withdrew into our caves, into our personal lives, into our sanctuaries of safety where we would no longer feel pain, no longer allow our emotions and visions to be wounded!

Many of us withdrew into a place where we would never allow that to happen to us again. Why would we ever walk through the pain of devastation again... that wouldn't be wisdom would it? Why would we ever allow the Lord to empower us with vision that could be thwarted or diverted? Why would God ever let us into relationships that may end up being the source for painful daily thought? I mean we had been family. Family is never supposed to go through those things... Family is meant to be together ... Family is meant to be perfect.

But it wasn't perfect, it was difficult, it was painful.... and yet we still retain the title of "family" ... regardless of whether we are broken, scattered, hurt, or over it! Some still hide in the caves! Some still lick their wounds! Some still nurture feelings of how it should have been!

To the devastated; to the hurt; to the scattered; to the sick heart; "Come Out! This is the day of Restoration!" The reason it hurt was because we are family. The reason we lost vision was because God entrusts vision to families, and when family is scattered vision wanes... fulfillment doesn't matter if your family is not there to enjoy it!

As you "suck it up"... and come out of the caves... as you walk out of the darkness where you thought you would be protected from seeing the vision He gave you... where you would be protected from the "family" you once thought He gave you... where you would be hidden from relationships and failure... when you step into the light of the day... you will see your vision there again...

you will see "family" again (older, wiser, with healed wounds and scars)... and a future and a hope.

It's time once again to embrace the future; embrace the vision and calling of God in your life... embrace His purpose and step into the light!

Then Eleazar the priest said to the soldiers who had gone into battle, "This is the requirement of the law that the LORD gave Moses:) Gold, silver, bronze, iron, tin, lead) and anything else that can withstand fire must be put through the fire, and then it will be clean. But it must also be purified with the water of cleansing. And whatever cannot withstand fire must be put through that water.
Numbers 31:21-23

When you pass through the waters, I will be with you; and when you pass through the rivers, they will not sweep over you. When you walk through the fire, you will not be burned; the flames will not set you ablaze.
Isaiah 43:2

You let men ride over our heads; we went through fire and water, but you brought us to a place of abundance.
Psalm 66:12

This generation that "walks on water" is a generation that has previously walked through water, through fire, through difficulty... through events that baptized them and transformed their very being into something they could not be before.

When we receive the baptism that comes from Jesus it is full of the Holy Spirit's power, but it is also a baptism of fire that cleanses, empowers, removes flesh and causes us to be different than when the process began!

Although I obviously believe in baptism in water, the imagery is very faint as to the transformation that occurs in a life that is totally and thoroughly immersed in the process of God.

Once we have walked through and received these difficulties without complaint, these immersions of God, these baptisms, we can once again face the dreams that God gave us that fell flat. We can without fear, embrace them again. We can run with them, look at them, contemplate them, ask God for His wisdom on how to remain free from bitterness and haunting darkness and continue in the light and freedom of forgiveness and His glorious Grace!

When they had finished eating, Jesus said to Simon Peter, "Simon son of John, do you truly love me more than these?" "Yes, Lord," he said, "you know that I love you." Jesus said, "Feed my lambs." Again Jesus said, "Simon son of John, do you truly love me?" He answered, "Yes, Lord, you know that I love you." Jesus said, "Take care of my sheep." The third time he said to him, "Simon son of John, do you love me?" Peter was hurt because Jesus asked him the third time, "Do you love me?" He said, "Lord, you know all things; you know that I love you." Jesus said, "Feed my sheep. I tell you the truth, when you were younger you dressed yourself and went where you wanted; but when you are old you will stretch out your hands, and someone else will dress you and lead you where you do not want to go."

John 21:15-18

Resist him, standing firm in the faith, because you know that your brothers throughout the world are undergoing the same kind of sufferings.

1 Pet 5:9

Peter walked with The One who had the most dramatic vision and purpose ever to be played out in history. His relationship with Jesus was incredible. His revelation on the Son of Man set the foundation for the Church... yet Peter evidently walked too close to Jesus, because it was the striking of Jesus that resulted in the greatest hurt Peter would ever experience. Peter had his complete hope and trust and future wrapped up in the vision that Jesus had. Peter could not see the value of the cross, he could not see the value of the breaking, he could not see the value of a vision that had to die and as a result he ran, he hid, he denied, he turned his back on the prophetic destiny and went fishing!

But Jesus wasn't finished with Peter, the vision was not complete, and Peter was a part of the vision! While Peter retreated to his fishing, Jesus found him and reissued a call to the original purpose. Peter was about to be restored to the original intent of God. His call was never a job as a fisherman.... He was never meant to be simply throwing a net over a boat... and although it was safe, although there were no requirements for relationships, although there were no ways he could have been hurt emotionally, it was not the destiny of God for him. Peter was intended to fish for men. He was called to walking with those who would hurt, and be hurt. He was called to relate and commit and dream and bring about the purposes of God in the lives of those around him. His future was meant to have struggles and God was determined to bring about His process in the life of Peter.

At an event on the beach Jesus re-issued the call to Peter. He called Peter out of his cave... and Peter came out! Peter embraced the painfulness that he too walked through, and in moving on found that ALL of his dreams and vision and purpose were still intact!

Peter's initial response to suffering and difficulty were , "That can't be God!" He was the one who rebuked Jesus when told about the cross. He was the one who saw suffering and ran away. He was the one who felt justified in lying about his relationship with Jesus because "bad things don't happen to good people!"

After his restoration and call on the beach, we find a very different Peter. When we read later the words of Peter in regard to suffering, they are words of maturity and experience. "Don't be surprised with suffering!" he says. [5] His wisdom to others in regard to suffering is, "Quit feeling sorry for yourself! Others are going through the same thing!"

Peter has grown. He has embraced the difficulty without a sense of pride or loss. He has seen the difficulty as the very process of God that will enable him to do the vision that God has placed before him.

Those who walk on water are those who have been baptized by it. To overcome a storm, you first live through the storm. To overcome the power of the flames, you first step into it's scorching heat. The greatest victory of Peter was not his ability to heal or touch lives, it was to embrace the vision of God out of his desperation and step forward into it.

This generation is stepping into their destiny out of the crucible of pain. They come as voices, not echoes. They have walked through the valley themselves, and have the experience of his restoration power, the experience of the still small voice that speaks in the midst of adversity. They have come out of the caves and are facing the same world, with a much more profound power and word than they have ever witnessed before. This generation is rising!

1. "the stuff" was a term coined by John Wimber of Vineyard during the 1980's. His understanding was that we get to do the things that Jesus did, not simply talk about it, or teach it. He used the term "stuff" as the works of Jesus.

2. (John 15:20) Remember the words I spoke to you: 'No servant is greater than his master.' If they persecuted me, they will persecute you also. If they obeyed my teaching, they will obey yours also.

3. Repeatedly Paul and Peter reiterate the subject of suffering. In each occasion there seems to be a sense of purpose and destiny in the suffering, and so it's not to be avoided, but rather embraced. (Eph 3:13 NIV) I ask you, therefore, not to be discouraged because of my sufferings for you, which are your glory. (Phil 1:29-30 NIV) For it has been granted to you on behalf of Christ not only to believe on him, but also to suffer for him, (30) since you are going through the same struggle you saw I had, and now hear that I still have. (1 Pet 2:19-23 NIV) For it is commendable if a man bears up under the pain of unjust suffering because he is

conscious of God. (20) But how is it to your credit if you receive a beating for doing wrong and endure it? But if you suffer for doing good and you endure it, this is commendable before God. (21) To this you were called, because Christ suffered for you, leaving you an example, that you should follow in his steps. (22) "He committed no sin, and no deceit was found in his mouth." (23) When they hurled their insults at him, he did not retaliate; when he suffered, he made no threats. Instead, he entrusted himself to him who judges justly.

4. See "When Bruised Reeds Break" the story of my personal restoration and the hope for returning many to their intended purposes in God

5. (1 Pet 4:12-16 NIV) Dear friends, do not be surprised at the painful trial you are suffering, as though something strange were happening to you. (13) But rejoice that you participate in the sufferings of Christ, so that you may be overjoyed when his glory is revealed. (14) If you are insulted because of the name of Christ, you are blessed, for the Spirit of glory and of God rests on you. (15) If you suffer, it should not be as a murderer or thief or any other kind of criminal, or even as a meddler. (16) However, if you suffer as a Christian, do not be ashamed, but praise God that you bear that name.

CHAPTER EIGHT

THE DOORBELL OF HEAVEN

he eyes of the LORD pass back and forth throughout the earth looking, seeking, desiring to be with those whose hearts are fully committed to him."

Those who walk on water often ring the doorbell of heaven. Heaven has waited for this generation that will not only attract the attention of The Father, but also keep His attention as he releases favor on them! These are those who aren't looking for a fleeting event of "goose bumps" in an hour or two long meeting. This generation is looking for the place where the Father can rest His feet, lay His head, and find His Joy in the midst of His people! These have found out that a life given to God is more than simply exposing God to a glimpse of their love for Him, it is being totally captured and mesmerized by His very Presence in pure and holy worship!

There is a place where we can be mesmerized by the Presence of the Lord. It's that holy place that Abraham found after talking with God, and remained "standing in the Presence of the Lord."[1] It's the place Moses found, when for forty days He was in a cloud with the Lord.[2] Paul expressed it as being caught up to the third heaven.[3] It was a place where the reality of God's realm overwhelms the natural realm that we are so accustomed to.

That place is entered into by the bold; those who dare to remain standing in the Presence of the Lord long after we have already discussed all the issues of our lives with God. It's the place that we enter into after we have received all that we have wanted out of our time with God. It's the place where God gets what He wants out of our time with Him. It's the place of mesmerizing worship and adoration of the love of our lives... it's the place where our thoughts, attitudes, opinions and dreams meet the God of All and simply rest and abide in His Presence, knowing that nothing is more important, nothing is more valuable than simply being with Him. It is that place of complete capture and enthrallment in the One we adore... it is the place we have all sought for, the place we have all wanted to get to, but the place so few of us enter, and when we do, it's so rare.

I have often wondered why this place is so indefinable and elusive. It can't be taught in seminars or conferences… it is birthed only in a heart. I have found that those who experience the depths and heights of worship are those who enter into that place.

One of them, an expert in the law, tested him with this question: "Teacher, which is the greatest commandment in the Law?"   Jesus replied: "'Love the Lord your God with all your heart and with all your soul and with all your mind.' This is the first and greatest commandment.

Matthew 22:35-38

It's a clear mandate… Love the Lord Your God …. It's worship, worship and more worship!

For many years, I have taught that Worship is the highest priority that we as Christians can have. I held that opinion for about twenty five years, knowing that the greatest commandment is to "love the Lord with all your heart!." Nothing should pre-empt our adoration of God… not teaching, not evangelism, not ministry … nothing!

Because of this foundation, I have encouraged worship everywhere I have gone, either by doing it, or by encouraging others to do it. Ask anyone who knows me what they think I'm called to… they will answer worship. It's what I breathe, what I love, what I long to do all the time!

Over the last couple decades it has been my hope that people would see it modeled and then do it. In actual fact, what I saw happening was not all that I had hoped to see. I became extremely frustrated when I realized that although modeling may have helped produce the "activity" that surrounds worship, very few were actually entering into that place of mesmerizing worship that I described, and fewer still could actually even see the value of "giving it all" in worship.

I wondered how people could hear and feel the Presence of God without entering that place of mesmerizing worship and being captured and enthralled by God. There were points in my frustration that I would criticize or judge.... knowing it was wrong, I asked the Lord for greater wisdom on how to lead people to Him not simply in song, but in worship.

The Church at large has developed incredible avenues for worship, so much so that worship has become the "hottest Christian music genre". Everywhere you turn, you hear "worship music". It is on television ads, all over the radio, in Wal-Mart, in theme parks. Worship music is everywhere! Worship music is being sung by the hottest Christian artists, and more and more are moving to this genre as the days go by. We get so excited when a song "crosses over" to the secular world somehow believing that now we are impacting the world, but they listen to the song with an unsaved mind, unaltered, and fit it in the category much the same way that we sing their songs to fit our world!

I remember when the only way I could get a Vineyard song was through an employee of Vineyard Christian Fellowship, in Yorba Linda California, singing songs into a cassette tape player, because they didn't have any recordings made at the time. I am not against worship recordings; I have many and have recorded some myself, and plan to record more. But I can hope that there is something beyond the fad that will immerse our world in passionate, holy worship of Jesus.

Today we have all the bells and whistles, we have the most elite projection and computer systems, we have the best sound systems money can buy, we have incredible world-class musicians, and singers whose voices are wonderful and anointed... but do we really have that place of mesmerizing worship? Do we have that place where we are captured more with the Father's presence than we are with the technical production?

I have been in a few services where the technical experience was perfect... afterwards I felt as if I had been in a major theatrical production, but I wasn't sure the producer was God. There is a numinous presence when He is around, and there is no technical expertise that can improve on that.

When I first witnessed these "worship events" I was very excited. I thought surely the "priority" of worship is taking place. All over the world people are singing to Worship CD's, all over the world the songs of love for Jesus are being sung... we did it... we had made worship a priority. As I now perceive the "move" to a "genre" of worship.... I discern that maybe what we were doing was inoculating a generation from the "real deal." Many have "learned" that a few songs strung together in words towards God is what God called worship... and in so doing, they are missing that mesmerization of Heaven that I spoke of earlier. They are missing the communion and the fellowship and the lifestyle of a heart passionately in love with God!

My journey carried me to the events of worship where I realized some visited heaven and some stayed on planet earth... nothing different was offered to either group. Some experienced ecstasy, the others experienced obligation. Then it hit me, I knew what was missing from their worship experience.

One of the deepest frustrations of worship leaders' and pastors' hearts is opening their eyes and realizing that they are worshipping alone. No one seems to get it. It becomes very easy to judge and wonder what on earth is wrong with these people who won't worship.

The revelation for worship that explodes came during a particular worship event. I had been in a number of churches, but there was one church in particular where the people seemed to be "there" in worship. I opened my eyes as I was leading worship and realized, "I've got to catch up with them!" They were already there. You could look at their faces and realize that "they were not in this world"... they were with Jesus...

I asked the Lord about it because I had been in places with great sound, great acoustics, great musicians, and where the "big boys" had led worship and not experienced what I experienced that night.

"Lord what's the difference?" His gentle reply spoke so specifically to me. "They expected me Danny, they didn't expect a concert, or perfect sound, or a name, or a style... they believed I would show up in their midst because they were showing up to worship me... they had faith to enter in, and because of that faith, they did!"

Years of frustration rolled off of me. As a worship leader and musician, I had always thought if I could muster a better song, a better "groove", more anointed musicians, better sound... then surely the people would enter in. I was very wrong.

God was not looking for better anything... he was simply looking for hearts given to Him in adoration, knowing they would be fulfilled by His Presence. 2 Chronicles 16:9 says that "...the eyes of the LORD pass back and forth throughout the earth looking, seeking, desiring to be with those whose hearts are fully committed to him."

"Without faith it is impossible to please God, because anyone who comes to him must believe that he exists and that he rewards those who earnestly seek him."
Hebrews 11:6.

Although I had taught that worship was the highest priority for a believer, I had mistakenly also taught that worship was the highest value for a believer's lifestyle. It is not. The Bible clearly gives us revelation as to the highest value we can have in our Christian Walk.

The Lord gently corrected me. He told me although it was the highest priority of what we must do, the higher value of what we must live out is faith ... because without faith we cannot please Him. It is not enough to simply sing songs in a demonstration of worship; we must believe He will reward our faith born worship with His Presence and His Power.

Faith is the activity that releases heaven. Faith changes music and lifestyle into worship. Faith releases the mesmerizing Presence of God that allows us to simply be sustained by Him.

When Jesus returns the question on His mind is "when the Son of Man comes, will he find faith on the earth?" [4] In fact, it's the only question we find that He will ask when He comes back! It's not, "is everyone singing worship songs and buying worship CD's, singing the latest and greatest?" The issue has nothing to do with outward demonstration of worship, but inward demonstration of faith that expects God to move.

It is not the songs that make worship; it is the heart that loves Him, the life that lives Him, the thoughts, attitudes, and opinions that are overwhelmed by Him. Without this small thing called faith, all our worship is simply a new genre of music that is acceptable to the church community... but with faith... the simplicity of our songs and lifestyle can move us to a place right in front of the King.

Living In The Place Of Expectation

This faith born worship is the Doorbell of Heaven. We can clamor and make noise; we can have great worship music, an incredible band, use the latest and greatest methods, songs, styles, and technology and never see inside the heart of God in worship.

When faith activates our worship it is born of the Spirit, it has wings to fly and the Presence of God fills the house. For those who have found this doorway into the mesmerization of God; it is no surprise that He is there!

We may all get excited when we see a cloud, haze or mist in the building during worship... but I have found that those who enter by faith are not exceptionally impressed as if something incredible has happened, they expected it in the first place! For many, their experience prior to seeing the cloud or haze or whatever, was far more meaningful and encouraging to them because they had entertained a visit, not with angels or signs, but with God.

"Of course God was going to be there, I entered His Presence through faith and worshipped Him, He promised to reward me. Why would it be such a huge thing that His Presence actually comes? Why should I think it unique that He heals and frees and manifests His Power, He promised He would if I believed it, and I did!"

It is also noteworthy to realize that to neglect this basic premise results in years of ineffective, courteous, religious habits that carry no promise of fulfillment and joy in His Presence. If we do not enter by faith, we will never make it to the Throne Room in worship... and we have totally missed it. We have missed the very location of God because "God inhabits the praises of His people." [5] We endeavored to find God, but we went to the wrong address!

As Hebrews put it, "but we are convinced of better things for you!" [6] Those water walkers are easy to recognize.... They want God... and they want to be found by God. They are the ones who are pressing through by faith... they believe that when they do, He will be there, and will reward them.

It's the reason we exist. It's the reason for your salvation. It's the reason you gather ... it's the reason you worship... not so that you can get to heaven... but so that He gets you! It's that place where we are captured and caught away for the Presence of the King!

Come, walk with me into the destination of faith, where God rewards, where God mesmerizes, where you can walk on water!

1. (Genesis 18:1-22) The LORD appeared to Abraham near the great trees of Mamre while he was sitting at the entrance to his tent in the heat of the day. (2) Abraham looked up and saw three men standing nearby. When he saw them, he hurried from the entrance of his tent to meet them and bowed low to the ground. (3) He said, "If I have found favor in your eyes, my lord, do not pass your servant by. (4) Let a little water be brought, and then you may all wash your feet and rest under this tree. (5) Let me get you something to eat, so you can be refreshed and then go on your way—now that you have come to your servant." "Very well," they answered, "do as you say." (6) So Abraham hurried into the

108

tent to Sarah. "Quick," he said, "get three seahs of fine flour and knead it and bake some bread." ... (16) When the men got up to leave, they looked down toward Sodom, and Abraham walked along with them to see them on their way. (17) Then the LORD said, "Shall I hide from Abraham what I am about to do? (18) Abraham will surely become a great and powerful nation, and all nations on earth will be blessed through him. (19) For I have chosen him, so that he will direct his children and his household after him to keep the way of the LORD by doing what is right and just, so that the LORD will bring about for Abraham what he has promised him." (20) Then the LORD said, "The outcry against Sodom and Gomorrah is so great and their sin so grievous (21) that I will go down and see if what they have done is as bad as the outcry that has reached me. If not, I will know." (22) The men turned away and went toward Sodom, but **Abraham remained standing before the LORD.**

2. (Exodus 24:18) Then Moses entered the cloud as he went on up the mountain. And he stayed on the mountain forty days and forty nights.

3. (2 Corinthians 12:2-4) I know a man in Christ who fourteen years ago was caught up to the third heaven. Whether it was in the body or out of the body I do not know—God knows. (3) And I know that this man—whether in the body or apart from the body I do not know, but God knows— (4) was caught up to paradise. He heard inexpressible things, things that man is not permitted to tell.

4. Luke 18:8

5. Psalm 22:3

6. (Hebrews 6:9 NASB) But, beloved, we are convinced of better things concerning you, and things that accompany salvation, though we are speaking in this way.

CHAPTER NINE

LEAPFROG AND THE KINGDOM

ll of you, clothe yourselves with humility toward one another, because, "God opposes the proud but gives grace to the humble." Humble yourselves, therefore, under God's mighty hand, that he may lift you up in due time."

1 Peter 5:5-6

"A man's wisdom gives him patience; it is to his glory to overlook an offense."

Proverbs 19:11

A number of years ago a "spiritual father" of mine shared a concept of Kingdom ministry and growth that has stayed with me. He said, "The Kingdom is like a "spiritual leapfrog" game. We are constantly being encouraged by others who may have been behind us before, but now are ahead of us. Our growth and maturity comes when we recognize that we are not always at the forefront, but must always be learning. Humility comes to those who can learn from sources that seem unlikely.

A few weeks ago, I shared with this precious spiritual father the various "stories" that are currently happening around the world. I recounted specific accounts of the "current" heroes of the faith who are seeing literally thousands and in some cases millions coming to Jesus, those who are seeing the miraculous power of God moving in greater measure than I have seen in my lifetime. I shared about goings on in my own life, and some of the lives around me and that I still wanted to pursue the things that I had so passionately pursued in my early years. I had seen numerous miracles through this man, and through those around his life. I asked him if the powerful release like that was still happening through his life and the individuals who were his colleagues. He indicated he had not seen that kind of profound release of the Spirit like that for many years. He continued to reflect that he believed the founder of that movement would still be pursuing those things if he were alive. He had a passion for seeing the authentic power of God released in the earth through the church... that is what so drew my heart to the vision he shared... I have the same heart... I so desire to see the full manifest release of authentic power of God exploding throughout the earth in saving, healing, miraculous intervention!

The next day John was there again with two of his disciples. When he saw Jesus passing by, he said, "Look, the Lamb of God!" When the two disciples heard him say this, they followed Jesus.

John 1:35-37

When do we realize we must again back up and step into a fresh revelation where God is once again humbling us to learn again? When do we realize the dead is dead, and the dead should bury it? Is it not the nature of Jesus to either raise the dead, or encourage those who are tending the dead that will not be raised to leave it?

"Good surfers know how to bale!" I heard a speaker at a conference share that statement and was reminded about a statement that actually catapulted me into the movement that was to be my home for almost fifteen years. My cousin, whose church had experienced profound release of God's power in South Africa, had shared a single phrase with me… "God has moved past the charismatic movement!"

It amazes me how we can remain satisfied with "enough" revelation of Jesus, when we are given the opportunity for a "greater" revelation of Jesus. John's disciples, following after the revelation they knew of God, quickly dropped the "Ministry of John" when they were given the opportunity to follow the greater "Ministry of Jesus."

My cousin's statement touched on the fact that we as individuals become very comfortable with what it was that God did, and so remain focused on trying to reconnect with those experiences and the emotions associated with "the Glory days" of our faith. We recount the stories of yester-year not realizing that God is on the move today and we need to be moving on with God, not remaining in a state of "holding onto the past." It's not that God doesn't do things through the past movements and traditions. God always moves where people love Him. He is always faithful, but we can become stagnant and lose the passion of our faith and love for God when we don't stay on the edge of looking for what the Father is doing today!

I was recently reflecting with some folk who had been a part of the church I had planted back in the 80's & 90's about what it was that God did during that time. They shared with me the incredible things that God did and how difficult it was for them to see anything today that compared with what we experienced back then.

I can concur that there were amazing things that did happen in that church, but I also must look at the follow up fruit from that experience and ask myself the difficult questions that church planters are required to ask. "Where are the people now?" "What are the relationships like now?" "Who fell through the cracks?" "Are the people who were a part of the experience still experiencing the power and passion of Jesus in their lives, are they still releasing healing and power through their lives and ministry, is worship still exploding through them as it did with us?" I found my answers. With a few it continues...

Now it is required that those who have been given a trust must prove faithful.

1 Corinthians 4:2

God has entrusted to us the fullness of the purposes of God. Those purposes were not completed when we came to faith, or when we found a wonderful church, or when we once experienced the fullness of His Presence. Those purposes are progressive, always moving forward, always on the cutting edge, always yet to be seen. When we simply maintain what once was, we miss the purposes of God and embrace a "faithless" world-view that requires no further risk and opportunity for greater demonstrations of God in our future.

Faithfulness, passion, and fruitfulness is not measured by periods of time, but over the length of a lifetime. I don't really care what we had... I want to have, and keep on having His Presence, His Power, His anointing in my life. If I don't experience that, it doesn't matter what I had, it didn't infect my whole life!

The secret of faithfulness is not maintaining the status-quo of our faith, but rather learning to move on with the Spirit of God. We are not called to a maintained faith, but to a vibrant, active outworking faith. James declares that faith that simply is maintained inactively is purposeless. [1] Faith must have a current demonstration if it is indeed to be counted as faithfulness. The ongoing activation of faith through our lives determines whether or not we are faithful.

But there is a generation that would trade all of the experiences we have had to have a current experience with Jesus! That is the delight of those who are following the Father! They never know what awaits them, but they know who directs them to the place of that future wonderful encounter with the God of the Open Heavens!

The book of Exodus recounts the story of the bronze snake in the desert that healed people. The event was a true, historical, profoundly miraculous experience. But it was also the source for later failure on the part of God's people. The spring that released healing, would eventually become the bog of toxic idolatry. [3]

Former victories and encounters that become idols in the present steal vision, purpose, hope and destiny out of people's lives! When something requires us to lay aside previous experiences of victory in order to encounter the present move of God, it can feel offensive to us. It is only when we humbly receive the offense of the present move of God that we will continue on in what God has called us to.

I can reflect back to "glory days" of an earlier church plant. I don't naively remember those days through rose colored glasses as some do. I recall that what we experienced was not always accepted by the establishment... we had articles written on us in newspapers, periodicals, and reports on TV and radio telling others to avoid this move! A local church actually did a weekend seminar instructing their parishioners to avoid us! It took a lot of courage to move into the things the Lord was doing back then... and it will take courage to move into the things that God is doing today and will do five years or ten years from now!

True teachability and humility comes when we receive the offense of a new move... when we realize that we may not be the place God is going to move next... and that we must move where He moves. The early church was constantly in the state of learning. When tongues of fire and new languages were released in a public meeting, the question was indeed, "What does this mean?" That activity had never occurred in any of their meetings. Later, they would again face similar questions when the Gospel was redeeming the lives of pagan Gentiles who were "accursed."

It was the norm for the early church to experience new things. And so should it be for us today. We should not be simply preserving old philosophies and paradigms of ministry and church life if God is initiating something fresh to the world today. The method of Jesus and the early church was to simply "ride the wave of the Father's purposes!"

Maybe, just maybe, the next move of God won't come out of our movement, or the denomination or group we are a part of! Maybe, just maybe, the next move of God will require our humility to suck up our personal opinions and ideas of how things should happen. And maybe, just maybe we will begin to see that God will "allow" us to participate in what He is doing, rather than us believing that if God will move, it will happen in our way, in our place, in our personality, in our style!

God is raising up a people who recognize the profound reality that God sits in the heavens and laughs! They have begun to understand that His ways are not ours. His thoughts are so much higher. His purposes? They will prevail! They have become comfortable with the uncomfortable. [2] They have embraced the very things that in some cases they have personally disdained, in order for the purposes of God to be in preeminence.

We are simply servants - servants called to follow the Lamb wherever He goes - in His way - in His style - in His purposes!

Lord... can I play leapfrog? Let me learn. Let the things that offend me be the source of growth that I can receive all that you have. Let me learn from those who I may not have noticed before - those you are raising up, who have fresh vision and who are seeing the Kingdom coming in power in ways unfamiliar to me, simply because you are moving in new and profound ways that I may not be comfortable with! Lord, let me catch this wave of what you are doing, and the waves that will occur in the future. Let me dwell in the place where the Father is always doing something!

That is where I want to be!

1. (James 2:14-18 NIV) What good is it, my brothers, if a man claims to have faith but has no deeds? Can such faith save him? (15) Suppose a brother or sister is

without clothes and daily food. *(16)* If one of you says to him, "Go, I wish you well; keep warm and well fed," but does nothing about his physical needs, what good is it? *(17)* In the same way, faith by itself, if it is not accompanied by action, is dead. *(18)* But someone will say, "You have faith; I have deeds." Show me your faith without deeds, and I will show you my faith by what I do.

2. (John 6:60-68 NIV) "On hearing it, many of his disciples said, "This is a hard teaching. Who can accept it?" Aware that his disciples were grumbling about this, Jesus said to them, "Does this offend you? What if you see the Son of Man ascend to where he was before! The Spirit gives life; the flesh counts for nothing. The words I have spoken to you are spirit and they are life. Yet there are some of you who do not believe." For Jesus had known from the beginning which of them did not believe and who would betray him. He went on to say, "This is why I told you that no one can come to me unless the Father has enabled him." From this time many of his disciples turned back and no longer followed him. "You do not want to leave too, do you?" Jesus asked the Twelve. Simon Peter answered him, "Lord, to whom shall we go? You have the words of eternal life."

3. (2 Kings 18:4) He removed the high places, smashed the sacred stones and cut down the Asherah poles. He broke into pieces the bronze snake Moses had made, for up to that time the Israelites had been burning incense to it. (It was called Nehushtan.)

CHAPTER TEN

THE TIME FOR REBELLION IS NOW

And the LORD was with him; he was successful in whatever he undertook. He rebelled against the king of Assyria and did not serve him.

2 Kings 18:7

It's everywhere. It can be seen all over the world infiltrating the love of God's Heart. It's not a good thing, but it appears successful and full of favor. It's called Babylon[1]... the King of Assyria... the pomp and circumstance, the incredible buildings, the vastness of expense and the focus of pride. Many of God's people are there... they are in exile there... and most don't even realize that they are in exile. After all it appears very successful ... it has the makings of acceptability and the "well oiled machine" is working well.

But I wonder... is it a form of Godliness without the power? [2]

"Appearances" are everything. To a world that has become astute at avoiding things of the Spirit, the natural mind "proves" that this appearance of everything good is 'god.' The problem is; to the spiritually discerning, to the spiritual mind, this appearance simply detracts people from that which is really good, the supremacy of His Power.

Is it for the system, the machine, the massive overwhelming ability to fit God into 30 or 60 minutes that Jesus spent a horrible day on a cross? Or was it for a people so empowered so equipped so full of His Glory and His Love that the darkest places of their lives would result in miraculous power in the lives of those around them? [3] When our shadows are affecting and infecting this world with the glorious majestic healing power of Jesus, then maybe we can say we are free from the King of Assyria and that we are no longer in exile. At that time, we can declare that we are following a new King who does not concern Himself with all the glory that we can muster, because we are bursting with the Glory and Love that surrounds Him and those who are close to Him!

"And from the days of John the Baptist until now the kingdom of heaven suffers violence, and violent men take it by force.

~Matthew 11:12 NASB

Unless you have relegated yourself to the walls of un-passionate faith, you like I can see that there is violence that is happening in the Kingdom of God. Amazingly, in the name of "peace" we fail to bring attention to the things that are disrupting the Peace of God, and so we acquiesce to the violence against the Kingdom and don't become the "peacemakers" that Jesus speaks of.[4]

All too often we are very careful not to make statements that might ostracize us from the "mainstream." I wonder what Elijah or John the Baptist would have done?

I don't have to wonder. I know what they did. They were more committed to the purposes of God than they were acceptability by the reigning religious folk. For both of them the costs were high. Elijah spent his life in obscurity by streams and with widows. John the Baptist spent his time in the desert and in jail before he was beheaded. They counted not their lives so much as to shrink from death.[5]

There is something of the nature of God that must come through during this hour. It is the explosion of truth and righteousness without regard for consequence. Without criticizing or judging His Bride, we must bring her forward from the obvious shortcomings into His Purposes for her.

I previously made mention of the bronze serpent that was erected during the great exodus. In that incredible account we learn of profound miraculous healing that was offered to the people of Israel who had been afflicted by a plague of snakes.[6]

It would take generations, but fixation around favorite traditions and memories always results in idolatry. The story unfolds under the reign of King Hezekiah. He had to eventually destroy the bronze snake as he did several other idols. [7] Hezekiah, through his righteous response, gained profound favor from the Lord, and as a result initiated a rebellion against Babylon. [8]

There was a rebellion. This was a holy rebellion that broke faith with "religious relics" and renewed allegiance to the Lord. There is an angst that is being released into this generation that stands before an open heaven. There is a righteous anger, as was expressed by Jesus in a Temple gone awry. It is a profound understanding that God desired far more, and far better, than we have become comfortable with. It is an awakening to the fact that so many have lost their way into the purposes of God, because they have not progressed in their faith... they have stagnated around the relics of past victories.

Worshipping events of the past has never been the heart of God for us. The worship of anything, even if it came from God, is always idolatry.

Worship itself can become a bronze snake. It is not worship that is the answer for the church and the world... it is, and always has been, only God. We only find God through the process of seeking God, pursuing Him, sometimes "using" worship as a means to express our love for Him, but always coming back to the simplicity that He alone is the answer. Singing worship songs without a passionate heart for God will not experience God, or release His power... sadly, it may only produce idolatry.

It is time for a holy rebellion to be birthed. Revolutionaries are rising all over the earth. There is no satisfaction for them in former answers, they seek the God who speaks today, they are the ones who are passionate seekers who want to find their refuge in God, alone!

1. (Dan 4:29-30 NIV) Twelve months later, as the king was walking on the roof of the royal palace of Babylon, (30) he said, "Is not this the great Babylon I have built as the royal residence, by my mighty power and for the glory of my majesty?"

2. (2 Tim 3:5 NIV) having a form of godliness but denying its power. Have nothing to do with them.

3. (Acts 5:15-16 NIV) As a result, people brought the sick into the streets and laid them on beds and mats so that at least Peter's shadow might fall on some of them as he passed by. (16) Crowds gathered also from the towns around Jerusalem, bringing their sick and those tormented by evil spirits, and all of them were healed.

4. (Mat 5:9 NIV) Blessed are the peacemakers, for they will be called sons of God.

5. (Rev 12:11 NIV) They overcame him by the blood of the Lamb and by the word of their testimony; they did not love their lives so much as to shrink from death.

6 . "The people came to Moses and said, "We sinned when we spoke against the LORD and against you. Pray that the LORD will take the snakes away from us." So Moses prayed for the people. The LORD said to Moses, "Make a snake and put it up on a pole; anyone who is bitten can look at it and live." So Moses made a bronze snake and put it up on a pole. Then when anyone was bitten by a snake and looked at the bronze snake, he lived."(Numbers 21:7-9)

7. (2 Kings 18:4) "he removed the high places, smashed the sacred stones and cut down the Asherah poles. He broke into pieces the bronze snake Moses had made, for up to that time the Israelites had been burning incense to it. t was called Nehushtan."

8. (2 Kings 18:7) "And the LORD was with him; he was successful in whatever he undertook. He rebelled against the king of Assyria and did not serve him."

CHAPTER ELEVEN

THE VISION JESUS HAS!

hrist loved the church and gave himself up for her to make her holy, cleansing her by the washing with water through the word, and to present her to himself as a radiant church, without stain or wrinkle or any other blemish, but holy and blameless.

Ephesians 5:25-27

If there is one thing I have witnessed in almost three decades of ministry, it is the fact that vision is critical to accomplishing purpose. We have all been quoted the passage, "...where there is no vision the people perish!" Most of us have also used that passage to promulgate our own ideas and thoughts about what should be taking place in our churches, our cities, our regions, our nation, or the world!

I think the most important question we must ask, if we are to be that generation that releases the authority of God with power, is the question: Whose vision are we to perpetuate?

I've seen the facilities, I've seen the motivations, I've seen the crowds, I've even seen some of the budgets. But is that the vision that Jesus had?

The vision that Jesus proposed to His disciples is often far different than we propose to ours. As a result, our success may be measured by standards other than Biblical standards. our ability to demonstrate the vision of Jesus is greatly diminished and in some cases is non-existent.

Jesus had a vision that was based more on qualitative results than quantitative. His goal was to make disciples throughout the earth. The emphasis was on *disciples* not converts. The goal of Jesus had to do with relationship[1], not membership. His goals were extremely idealistic and involved faith not means.

I would venture to say that Jesus sees the purpose of the church vastly different from what we normally express as Christian Faith in our western culture.

Primarily the vision that is commonly expressed by leaders of the church is something institutional or a formulation of methods that cause us to rally around a few priorities and values... these usually evolve into structures that may or may not have Biblical Values. Jesus' focus has nothing to do with what we do, but who we are.

The goal of Vision is to bring the Church into a place where it is "becoming" a "Bride" not just another "effective" organization. The vision of Jesus for the church was to produce something that was holy, clean, presentable, radiant, stainless, wrinkle-free, and unblemished. It sounds more like a laundry request than an organization. That's because it is. The focus for Jesus was never what we could accomplish, but who we would become! The mission he gave us to do was to represent Him with full brilliance, full power, full love, full evidence of His Kingdom!

So how do we understand the vision of Jesus?

"You are the Christ, the Son of the living God." Jesus replied, "Blessed are you, discerning proclaiming child of a Dove, for this was not revealed to you by man, but by My Father in heaven. And I tell you that you are a rock larger than a millstone... and on this rock I will build my church, and the gates of Hades (the grave) will not overcome it. I will give you the keys of the kingdom of heaven; whatever you bind on earth will be bound in heaven, and whatever you loose on earth will be loosed in heaven."

Matthew 16:16-19

Peter had an encounter, not with information, but with revelation. It was not enough to simply witness the miraculous, to know truth, or even to be a disciple of

Jesus. (Peter was the only one who received that revelation!) It was this revelation that released faith in Him..

Without Revelation, there can be no faith, and without faith, we can't please God. So Revelation becomes foundational to understanding the vision of Jesus. When we have a Revelation of Jesus, we also have a revelation of His Purposes and His Vision for our lives.

When there is no supernatural encounter, pursuing "vision" is simply pursuing a "good idea", but not necessarily a "God idea!" After an encounter with Jesus, and after the Revelation has been given, then vision which may be unseen for the moment, is determined already!

Evidently the early disciples operated out of a Revelation of "being with Jesus,"[2] and it was reflected throughout their lifestyle to such a degree that others took note, not of the information within them, but rather the relationship that they held and the manifestation of that relationship through their lives.

The whole of our Christian Walk is to be determined by this Revelation that releases Vision into Destiny and Purpose for our lives.

It was this understanding of the vision of Jesus that took the disciples from destiny seekers to vision fulfillers. They realized that if Jesus was the source for the vision, it was as good as done. Others evidently also understood this revelation. The centurion who came to Jesus and asked for healing for his daughter simply by a proclamation of Jesus, drew praise from Jesus because he understood well the purposes and vision of God in regard to sickness. [3]

Becoming a functioning disciple of Jesus who releases the Kingdom of God with power eliminates the mistaken belief that we can "try it" and see if it works. Faith doesn't allow for "trial runs," faith demonstrates God's ability through obedient servants who understand His purposes for men. True faith will hold on to that which is apparently contrary to the visible eye, and declare boldly what is only visible to the Spirit's intent. [4]

I liken faith to the high platform diver at the circus who looks at the little pool below with utmost confidence that he can dive the staggering drop to the tiny pool below, until he realizes that there is no water in the pool. He then requests that water be placed into the pool so that he can jump. The response through the bullhorn is "I will fill it up on your way down!" It seems to me this is most often how the Lord calls us by faith. To Abraham it was go where you have never been. To Enoch it was take a walk on the "spirit" side. To Noah, build something you have never seen. To Joshua walk around the walls of Jericho, they will fall.

On every occasion, faith was demonstrated through the apparent foolishness of radical obedience. To those who have seen the vision of Jesus, there is a revelation that anything less than radical obedience would result in missing the joy of God's intervention in the lives of His people. Anything less than complete reckless faith will cause us to be less than what God intended for us, because His destiny for us is wrapped up in His vision for this world.

During some meetings in New England I was pulled onto my own personal diving board. This one seemed higher than many I had been on. We had just reached the place in the service where "ministry time" was apparent. The worship was good, the message came out adequately, and the atmosphere was pregnant with Him! I was so excited to see what God was going to do.

"Tell them to take our their cell phones!"

I heard it, but I couldn't believe it. Was God actually asking me to have people take out their cell phones in church. I was always taught to turn them off!

I hesitated longer than usual and then blurted out. "If you have a cell phone please take it out and call people who are sick. Don't tell me their condition, I believe God will reveal it and heal them!"

I wanted to pull the words back into my mouth. My favorite prayer was engaged. "Oh God, Oh God, Help!"

After getting over the shock of what I had just asked them, the people started turning the church facility into an airport waiting room. Phones and ring tones went off throughout the room. The atmosphere was certainly not "ministry time" anymore.

A couple minutes went by and then a young man raised his hand. "I've got mine!, " he said. Great, he didn't even tell me if it was a man or a woman.

I began speaking. "It's a woman, you were in a car wreck three weeks ago. Your neck is in pain as well as your shoulders, but the Lord is healing it right now!"

The young man began weeping as he spoke into the phone. "Mom, did you feel that? Did that really happen?" He blurted out, "She says the pain is all gone!"

About a half hour later two women made their way into the meeting that was still going on. Several miracles had occurred that morning. The woman with the healed neck came up to me and said, "I'm the woman who was in the car wreck!" She rotated her neck around and around, free from pain. The other older woman just watched in awe.

The older woman was her mother from Europe. She didn't speak english, so through her daughter asked a question. "I have never met a God that heals. My daughter was in so much pain, can I meet this God?"

A few minutes later not only was she saved, but her blind right eye was healed as well as tumors in her stomach.

Every occasion of the release of the Kingdom is intended to spark faith. We are to look for the difficult cases. God is not limited to short diving boards... He loves the real high ones!

And without faith it is impossible to please God, because anyone who comes to him must believe that he exists and that he rewards those who earnestly seek him.

Hebrews 11:6

1. John 15 expresses the heart of Jesus for relationship above everything else.

2. Acts 4:1)They were surprised and wondered how easy it was for Peter and John to speak. They could tell they were men who had not gone to school. But they knew they had been with Jesus.

3. Matthew 8:8-10 The centurion replied, "Lord, I do not deserve to have you come under my roof. But just say the word, and my servant will be healed. {9} For I myself am a man under authority, with soldiers under me. I tell this one, 'Go,' and he goes; and that one, 'Come,' and he comes. I say to my servant, 'Do this,' and he does it." {10} When Jesus heard this, he was astonished and said to those following him, "I tell you the truth, I have not found anyone in Israel with such great faith

4. Luke 8:49-50 While Jesus was still speaking, someone came from the house of Jairus, the synagogue ruler. "Your daughter is dead," he said. "Don't bother the teacher any more." {50} Hearing this, Jesus said to Jairus, "Don't be afraid; just believe, and she will be healed."

5. 1 Corinthians 3:18 Do not deceive yourselves. If any one of you thinks he is wise by the standards of this age, he should become a "fool" so that he may become wise.

CHAPTER TWELVE

CONVERTS OR DISCIPLES

hrist loved the church and gave himself up for her to make her holy, cleansing her by the washing with water through the word, and to present her to himself as a radiant church, without stain or wrinkle or any other blemish, but holy and blameless."

Ephesians 5:25-27

Convert. It literally means "an arriver from a foreign region", someone who "complies with the teachings." It's really what most of us have been taught is the focus of the church. We have learned adequately to go make converts; to go get others to say a prayer; to go get others to come to our thing. Go get them and make sure they sit through our meetings, get them to the point where they "look" like one of us!

Significantly, that word is NEVER used for a believer, never used for one of Jesus' own. Because Jesus doesn't have any converts - He only has disciples.

The focus of Jesus was never to get people "in church" but to have them "follow Him". His goal is not that they "look like" one of His, but rather that they ARE one of His!

The Word does speak about conversion, but it is not necessarily a good thing! Jesus warns the Pharisees that they are experts in conversion, to the downfall of the convert!

"Woe to you, teachers of the law and Pharisees, you hypocrites! You travel over land and sea to win a single convert, and when he becomes one, you make him twice as much a son of hell as you are." [1]

What a wonderful commendation for the role of making converts! The Vision of Jesus, is not a vision of multitudes of converts! In fact, I'm not sure Jesus is very impressed when we can fill every seat in a place to "prove" that we are doing our part in fulfilling our vision of reaching the world. Jesus is looking for Disciples! He is looking for those who walk like Him, sound like Him, know His Father like Him, and release His Ministry like Him!

One of the most often quoted passages of Scripture has been utilized repeatedly to make converts, when in fact it was given to make disciples. Jesus said, *"go and make disciples of all nations, baptizing them in the name of the Father and of the Son and of the Holy Spirit, and teaching them to obey everything I have commanded you. And surely I am with you always, to the very end of the age."* [2]

The intent of Jesus was this word "Disciple." It carries with it a connotation that this is a teachable pupil learning not only how to articulate the teachings of the teacher, but also do and accomplish the same activities of the teacher.

Jesus' vision is that we "make" disciples. His vision is that revolution transpires in the lives of His own. That He can find a resting place in another life. That not only will the "knee bow" but also the tongue confess, and the life live and express Jesus in all aspects! It is a metamorphosis accomplished by His overwhelming Love and an encounter with Him, not simply a conformation based upon knowledge

Jesus' vision is not for people to recite a prayer. His vision is not simply for people to receive "tickets" out of hell. His vision is not simply that someone can recall walking down an aisle somewhere. The Vision of Jesus is that a life experiences revolution, something so significant that it could never be confused with the former state. His desire is something that is so radically different from it's former state that every facet of life changes. That's a disciple. It's someone who not only knows Jesus, but looks, acts, and does the works that Jesus did.

Recently a relative of one of our team came to a meeting as an unsaved, unseeking lost man. He was dying of cancer and as a result had lost salivary glands through radiation treatment. He also had lost the ability to eat and a tube was inserted into his stomach to feed him. He came simply because my friend Jim invited him. I didn't know anything about him, nor did I meet him.

During most of the first meeting he simply sat there stunned by the explosive worship and wondering what he was doing there. The Lord spoke to me that there was someone there who had cancer that needed healing. When I shared it, he responded and received prayer from a couple that night. The next two weeks he returned and received prayer from many in the meeting, experiencing the increasing Love of Jesus through each of those that prayed for him. The following week he went to his doctor who indicated that his salivary glands were totally healed. An medical impossibility according to him. The man shared the story of the previous three weeks of meetings he had attended where he recieved prayer. The doctor was amazed and encouraged him to stay connected to the people who prayed for him, saying "They are good people!" The tube was removed and he was totally healed and had Christmas dinner with his family the following week.

A month later, before ever having said a normal "conversion" prayer, he was on the streets ministering to the poor out of his own bank account. Several months later he was ministering with great effectiveness to both new and old Christians. He had an encounter. That encounter saved Him much like Zacchaeus was saved in his encounter with Jesus. He became a disciple, as a result of a revelation of Jesus.

The message we carry will demonstrate this revelation of Jesus, or it will only produce earth walkers.

1 Matthew 23:15

2 Mathew 28:19-20

CHAPTER THIRTEEN

TAUGHT OR EMPOWERED

*T*hen they came to the crowd, a man approached Jesus and knelt before him. "Lord, have mercy on my son," he said. "He has seizures and is suffering greatly. He often falls into the fire or into the water. I brought him to your disciples, but they could not heal him." "O unbelieving and perverse generation," Jesus replied, "how long shall I stay with you? How long shall I put up with you? Bring the boy here to me." Jesus rebuked the demon, and it came out of the boy, and he was healed from that moment. Then the disciples came to Jesus in private and asked, "Why couldn't we drive it out?" He replied, "Because you have so little faith. I tell you the truth, if you have faith as small as a mustard seed, you can say to this

mountain, 'Move from here to there' and it will move.
Nothing will be impossible for you."

Matthew 17:14-20

Something different is occurring in this generation of believers. The gap between those who want to carry on playing church and those who don't is widening. With incredible speed the Lord is fanning the flame of His Heart in us. Some choose to become a bonfire, while others have chosen to hide from the wind in their buildings.

A number of years ago I worked with a church that had two very distinct factions in it. The experience, although necessary for my growth, was not enjoyable. One group wanted the Holy Spirit and all that comes with it, the other wanted the Church buildings, the heritage of their history, and their "correct" doctrine. Amazingly, these two groups had lived under the same roof for about ten years, living with the tension, and growing resentments. Prior to my role their, I was informed by the previous pastor who had been there for most of those years, that it was not a safe place for anyone who really wanted to move on with God. He had left, frustrated that the people never fully immersed themselves in the things of the Spirit of God.

As I looked at the two groups I realized that each of them were sincere and zealous for their particular belief system. One wanted "religion" sincerely, and actually declared they didn't want the Holy Spirit in their church. The other wanted the Holy Spirit in the church, to the degree that He could embellish and enhance their vision for what the church should look like. It would take me three years to discern that really each simply wanted control, and that when God is moving in a situation, He is the only one in control, we must relinquish that to Him.

As I began pondering the situation, I realized that there was something of God's destiny that He was desiring to pull out of the people on both sides that neither had experienced. It was His vision for that congregation, it was moving away from perversion and into destiny.

Pervert. Rebellious. Faithless. Why would Jesus use such strong words with His disciples? These are some of the strongest words He ever uses. Perverse? The word means morally corrupt and turned away from the truth! Jesus, don't you realize that the disciples were at least trying to get rid of the demon? Perverse? Why are they perverse? They were following you and trying to do what you were doing. Perverse? If they were perverse, than what am I? I surely have my times of failure in ministry too.

Our reaction to the verdict of Jesus is simply our misunderstanding of God's purposes for our lives. Perversion is anything in our lives that is less than the purposes God intended for us. It is deliberately not measuring up to the standard and calling He has set for us. We know that adultery, homosexuality, and the like are "perversions", but how is attempting to release the activity of the Kingdom equated with perversion? Is it possible that these two activities are kin of twisted morals?

The disciples had been given the Vision of Jesus. In fact a few of them literally had witnessed Jesus transfigured before them. His glorious nature and presence was known to the disciples. His activity of healing and deliverance was always successful, and it was intended to be that way. Jesus had already given them power and authority to rid the oppressed of demons and heal their diseases, but they were not releasing it in the same manner that He had equipped them to do so. They were not operating in the power that was their destiny. They were knowingly living out a substandard, uninspired, and deficient lifestyle void of the rife power of God.

Jesus' Vision is "His" church as an empowered radiant church that "is greater" than His earthly ministry. *"I tell you the truth, anyone who has faith in me will do what I have been doing. He will do even greater things than these, because I am going to the Father." (John 14:12)*

What Jesus foresaw for those disciples was entering into the "purpose" that God had for them. He didn't intend for them to enter into a perverted "purpose", but the authentic purpose of God! The purpose that is His objective is one that is full of power, full of destiny, full of the genuine authority of Christ.

This kind of authority Jesus gives only to His own, not to cerebral, fallow converts with head knowledge and religiosity to impress the intellect. This kind of Power sets others free and brings them out of darkness into the light, replacing heady knowledge with intimate relationship.

When Jesus touches a man or woman He goes far beyond an intellectual pursuit of knowledge, He brings them into an experiential knowledge of God where revolution transpires in the lives of others and disciples are made!

When true disciples are made, the Father finds His place of rest, knowing that His 21st Century disciples are continuing to release the ministry of Jesus on the earth. These understand their purpose. These are not perverts. Because the blind see, the lame walk, the dead are raised, and the poor hear good news. These walk on water. These are full of the power of Heaven and the world can see through them the demonstration of God, not with words, but with Power!

1. Matthew 23:15

2. Matthew 28:19

CHAPTER FOURTEEN

THE DOUBLE PORTION ANOINTING

$\mathcal{A}$bout 900 years prior to the release of the Holy Spirit at Pentecost, [1] there was another hungry disciple who realized that unless God moved in ways greater than He had before, it really was not worth the ride. His name was Elisha. It was his passion and hunger that this fledgling generation carried deep within their souls.

Elijah, the great prophet of old, the one who bearded kings had reached the zenith of his career and was ready to quit. In fact, he went to God begging for retirement and God allowed him to set up his departure. He was given three tasks, but his heart was already weary, and he completed only one. [2] Although commissioned to anoint kings, he only anointed one. A no-name, future

prophet, Elisha. He would later complete the tasks
originally given to Elijah.

Elijah, although used mightily in the past, had quit. He
was full of stories that were old and powerful, they
demonstrated to Elisha that God had moved in power
in history, but the passion and hunger in his heart would
only grow with each day that he spent with the retired
prophet. There were no more miracles… only two signs
left, one that would consume people with fire, the other
a chariot of fire when he would leave the earth.

The day finally came where Elijah recognized clearly that
his time had come. It was time for him to meet his maker.
What ensues, is a dramatic display of hunger and passion
in the life of Elisha. His remarkable hunger and passion
for a display of God is found as he begins the final journey
of Elijah.

Elijah must have spent much time sharing about the
miracles that had occurred through his life during the
"glory days." The legendary accounts must have left
Elisha wondering where that God was who released such
amazing power that the dead were raised and the
heavens opened.

Where on earth was this God of Elijah? Where was the
God that manifested Himself through healing and
demonstrations of mercy? Where was the God who
made it rain during drought? Where was the God who
provided by ravens? Where was the God that challenged

the idols of the day? Where was the God who raised the dead?

"Elijah, if I'm your apprentice, then show me the stuff, don't tell me the stories!"

The journey begins at Gilgal.

Gilgal was the first destination of the people of Israel when they entered the Promised Land. The events that take place there are prophetic fulfillment of historical proportions.

Gilgal was the place where the people of God "entered into their rest." Gilgal was the place where circumcision happened. Where sin was removed. For twenty-first century believers, it is entering into the Kingdom of God. It was the place of salvation, where the flesh was cut away and died, and where a new holy people emerged. The past was beyond the Jordan in the wilderness, buried with sin and unbelief. The present would find a new people emerging to apprehend the promises of God.

It was the event that would transform the people from wanderers and gatherers into warriors and destiny people. It was an awesome reflection on the transformation provided by God's merciful grace.

Stay at Gilgal Elisha!

Elijah, I've been to Gilgal. I've been circumcised, set apart, and have experienced the entry point of salvation.

I believe the day has come to move on in maturity to God's purposes for my life! I'm going anywhere you go. You have experienced more. You've shared the stories, you've seen it happen through your life. I want it for me!

Elijah and Elisha continue their walk towards the first stop on the journey.

Bethel.

Just the name sends powerful hope in our hearts! House of God. The Presence of God. Bethel became Bethel when Jacob slept there. It was the place where the heavens opened. It was the manifestation of an open heaven experience that resulted in a changed man and a future destiny with God. Bethel is a good place to stay.

Much of the "tongues talking" church today loves Bethel. It's profoundly evident. We reflect on the stories of powerful open heaven experiences that servants have had. Our history of these experiences is complete. We have followed the experiences of others who encountered God at Bethel. We have vicariously tasted heaven without experiencing the transformation that it brings.

Bethel was not only the place to inquire of God, it was the place where God responded. [3] Bethel was the place where the prophets had their school. [4] It was a place of incredible learning and teaching.

"Stay at Bethel Elisha!"

Elijah, I've been to Bethel. I've heard the prophetic words. I have experienced prophetic events. I watched the prophets prophecy to one another repeatedly. I've seen them develop their skills and become incredibly gifted in hearing the voice of God. I've heard the eloquent stories and experiences, but I know that there is more! I can't stay at Bethel. I want to experience my destiny, not just hear more about what it will be.

The two journeyed on and came to the place remembered as the conquest of God!

Jericho.

It's the place of Revival. It's the place of the miraculous. It's the guardian to the Promised Land. It lies in the fields of Harvest. It's the fortress of the enemy undone and demolished by simple obedience to a ridiculous command. It's the place where the walls fall, and God is glorified. Jericho is an incredible place to be.

There was no single battle in Scripture that approached the victory of Jericho. A people apprehending their promise would defeat the enemy with weapons unknown to this world! This is the prophetic version of a sweeping move of God released by His Spirit. History has recorded them over and over. The Joshua's of the church were the Finney's, the Wesley's, the Whitefield's and so many others! The scene of Jericho has been played out through the centuries by the obedient and we have witnessed the Great Awakenings, the Welsh Revival, the Azusa Street

Revival, the Toronto Blessing, and the Brownsville Outpouring.

It's good here Elisha. Here you can remain clothing yourself in history and moves of God, where you can enjoy all that God has done!

I am sure that Elijah's encouragement to Elisha at this point reaches a profound disgust with Elisha. I can imagine that Elisha simply responded with the same frustration that many in this generation are so profoundly vocalizing. "I don't care what happened back there. I want it here. I don't care that they did it. I want to do it!"

Stay at Jericho. Never. The cost to remain status-quo is too high. I would die of boredom as I recounted the stories of others, but didn't have my own to tell. My testimony is important. I overcome the enemy by the Blood of the Lamb AND the word of MY testimony.

Elijah, wherever you go, I am going! I have to have what you have experienced. I have to know it experientially, not just vicariously!

The form of two men now standing on the banks of the Jordan. The banks that represent the boundaries of the very promises of God! The verge of God's Destiny! On the other side of this river, the wilderness, the place of wandering, the place where the only valid response is "how do I get back in?"

Elisha, this is where we part. Stay here. You are in the promise. Your inheritance has already been secured by others who have gone on ahead of you. They have provided the place for you to simply enjoy the fruit of their labor. You're anointed. You have a historical anointing passed on to you from servants of old. You have your whole life ahead of you! Stay here. Watch from a distance, I have to go meet my Maker.

Elijah, you don't seem to understand. I want this for myself. I can't experience the fullness of the anointing that Joshua operated in, that Moses held and that eclipses the normal "anointing" that is on his people by virtue of their history. I will take that anointing, but I want the second anointing, the one that alters history, the one that frees nations, the one that causes the dead to rise and leprosy to flee! I want a double portion anointing of what you have. I want more than what you have experienced. I want to go further than you did, and see the Glory days continue long after I am dead!

In order for me to have that anointing, I must find myself in the same predicament as those who tasted that anointing. I must first walk "out of the promise" in order to apprehend it for myself. I don't simply want the anointing that others have... I want something more. I want to apprehend the promises just like Joshua and the people who walked across this river bed on dry ground did. I want to see the God of Elijah that you talk about and the only way for me to see it, is to go out there with you! I'm coming with you!

The mantle falls across the mighty river and the water is wrenched back by the Hand of God revealing the ancient path that once saw the feet of over a million. [5] In the distance those who are satisfied with the status-quo watch two cross the dry river bed and climb to the safety of the far shore just as the water plummets down in torrential crash and becomes a flowing river again. They remark how incredible it was to have witnessed the faith of these two bold men, and wondered why those kind of events never happened in their lives.

Elijah?

Yes, Elisha.

I want twice what you have been allowed to carry.

Are you sure?

Do you know what you are asking for?

I want a double portion.

If you can see me when I am taken, you will be given that stewardship.

The eyes of Elisha are about to be branded, and he doesn't realize it. Years later he would lay hands on another servant who couldn't see God's world and he would see.

His hunger carries him in a spiritual realm to see the world that is not evident to the natural mind, and he sees chariots of fire catching Elijah up on the journey back to his Maker.

He sees it and cries. "I see it! I see the chariots of fire! I can see the realm of God! My eyes have been baptized by this revelation and now I will never see anything in the same way again!"

The mantle falls from Elijah's shoulders, not just in the natural, but in the spirit. It was Elijah's mantle of authority, but it was Gods' anointing that Elisha received because of passionate pursuit. Elisha picks it up, and with new eyes, with new anointing, with new destiny he recalls the stories of old and presses in for his own story to begin!

One last time the frustration is revealed in the words of Elisha as he recalls the accounts of Elijah's Glory days. His words ring through the night. "Okay God, I've heard all the stories I want to hear. I'm no longer satisfied to stay in the shadow of someone else's anointing watching them do what you told me I could do. Where is that God who moved in power? Where is the God who sets the earth trembling? Where is the God of Elijah? It is Him that I want as my own. It is He that I wish to see and follow. It is THAT God that I want to come here and now! Oh, Where is the Lord God of Elijah?"

The mantle falls in the direction of the promise. Twice in one night the rivers are bridled by the Hand of God and

Elisha begins to enter into his destiny. The double portion fits him well... it was birthed from passion and hunger ... the motives were pure.

In the distance those who are satisfied with the status-quo watch one cross the dry river bed and climb to the safety of the promised land just as the water plummets down in torrential crash and becomes a flowing river again. They remark how incredible it was to have witnessed the faith of this man, and wondered why those kind of events never happened in their lives.

That anointing rested... all of his days. In fact, after he died, the anointing continued to rest. Passion and hunger for the things of God release anointing long after a lover of God is gone. At least a year after Elisha would meet his Maker his bones would raise a dead man to life.

That's what hunger for more of God does. It produces life in everything around it. The anointing remains in the bones.

The frustration of this generation to see God move in power is the frustration of Elisha, and God sees it and hears it. The frustration is captivating to God and the angels because for the first time in generations there are those who are willing to lay down all and follow hard after God regardless of the status-quo, regardless of acceptance, regardless of price! They are willing to pay the price to see God move.

Many of them have already stepped outside the promises of God in order to step back in with authority and power. Some have willingly laid down the "status-quo" church life, in order to experience the "God invaded life!" For them, there is no future in simply reproducing what doesn't bear lasting fruit, they desire the destiny of heaven... they desire the "Greater Works" of Jesus.

Elisha never passed on his mantle. Jesus picked it up, and encouraged his disciples with these words. You are going to do greater things than the things you have seen. [6] You stand in the lineage of Elisha. The double portion is yours. All you have to do is void your way of doing it, count the cost, and apprehend it.

The Jordan is waiting for a few, daring servants who have heard enough stories and want to experience God!

Maybe you have found yourself outside the "promised land" and for some reason do not even care to be in the "promised land" without the evidence of God! Maybe you have followed Elijah unwittingly past all the former miracles, past all the former experiences, past all the historical events into the land beyond the promise... the wilderness... where the only obvious, the only valid response is "how do I get back in to the Promised Land WITH the Power of the Almighty flowing through me?"

This could be your day to begin crying out... I've heard it all before Lord... I'm frustrated with the stories of years gone by. I'm weary with hearing about how others are experiencing your Presence and Power in their lives! I want your power in me. I want you to release heaven through me. I want to see the miraculous happen through me. I want to see the Might of Heaven released on this earth all around me. I am calling on YOU OH LORD GOD OF ELIJAH!

1 .Acts 2

2. 1 Kings 19:15-17- The LORD said to him, "Go back the way you came, and go to the Desert of Damascus. When you get there, anoint Hazael king over Aram. 16 Also, anoint Jehu son of Nimshi king over Israel, and anoint Elisha son of Shaphat from Abel Meholah to succeed you as prophet. 17 Jehu will put to death any who escape the sword of Hazael, and Elisha will put to death any who escape the sword of Jehu.

3. Judges 20:18

4. 2 Kings 2:3

5. estimated by several scholars

6. John 14:12 - I tell you the truth, anyone who has faith in me will do what I have been doing. He will do even greater things than these, because I am going to the Father.

CHAPTER FIFTEEN

THE EXPECTATION OF FRUIT

*S*eeing in the distance a fig tree in leaf, he went to find out if it had any fruit. When he reached it, he found nothing but leaves, because it was not the season for figs. Then he said to the tree, "May no one ever eat fruit from you again." And his disciples heard him say it… In the morning, as they went along, they saw the fig tree withered from the roots. Peter remembered and said to Jesus, "Rabbi, look! The fig tree you cursed has withered!"

Mark 11:13-14, 20-21

Picture this event. Jesus has been with the disciples for several years. In fact, His human earthly ministry is all but finished. The disciples have come to know Him as extremely compassionate and loving. His ministry has always been for restoration. To the blind He gives sight. To the dead, life! Rebellious storms are brought to peace. The hungry are fed. Never has something negative been produced by Jesus. Jesus is all positive until....

Jesus comes upon a fig tree that is barren, reasonably barren, it is not the season for fruitfulness! The event of this tree is a significant digression from all of the other miracles of Jesus. For many years I wondered why this story was included in the Bible.

Jesus, why did you curse the poor fig tree? It was out of season. You know what a season is. Don't you?

Jesus' activity demonstrates the purposes of God in regards to seasons. "What's a season?"

It doesn't make a lot of sense until you look at some other trees in Scripture.

 "And the LORD God commanded the man, "You are free to eat from any tree in the garden."

(Genesis 2:16)

What a glorious garden it was. Made for man, made for God. It would be the joy of heaven to walk through that garden day after day, talking and laughing and sharing life with man. Eden was a wonderful time in the History of God. It was here where His perfect purpose was created! God couldn't create anything outside of His purposes, He couldn't make something that was in error... the Garden was perfect!

Daily, God would walk with Adam and Eve in the garden. I can imagine that in the interaction during those walks and fellowship, God would partake of the fruit of the trees in the garden along with Adam and Eve. He created it. It was very good! Why wouldn't He eat it?

God didn't create anything that was dead at any time. Everything He made was vibrant with life. In fact fruit, seed, and life are marks of the Presence of God! Not only did God enjoy fruitful trees in the Garden, His blueprint for His and our future is adorned with a tree. " On each side of the river stood the tree of life, bearing twelve crops of fruit, yielding its fruit every month. And the leaves of the tree are for the healing of the nations." [1]

Trees under the purposes of God bear fruit without regard for season, ever!

When Jesus looked for fruit on that poor little fig tree, He was looking through the eyes of eternity. He was looking into the intended destiny of God for that tree. It failed to reflect the destiny of God, and therefore was not fit to take up space.

My theology went into a tailspin. I began realizing that so much of what I had taught through the years had to do with various "seasons" that we were walking through. I was now realizing that God was not as committed to a "season" theology as I was. Paul writes to Timothy, "Preach the Word; be prepared in season and out of season; correct, rebuke and encourage—with great patience and careful instruction. "[2]

Evidently, the final "season' in our lives comes when we step out of darkness, and into the light. Paul again writes to Titus, "at his appointed season he brought his word to light through the preaching entrusted to me by the command of God our Savior". Subsequent to salvation… seasons stop. The New Day arrives. We are now living in the "Day of the Lord!"

When Jesus went to the fig tree, He expected to see fruit, not based upon "fallen reality" but based on "eternal reality", and in so doing set the precedent for all of us who will enter into the destiny that God has for us. It is ALWAYS the season for fruit! There is no season of barrenness in the Kingdom, only aberrations of our own unbelief.

When we respond to the "natural" world with what we would consider common sense, we miss the "supernatural" world that operates by faith… and is the realm that God intended for us to live in. It is an anomaly that we operate on a level less than what God planned for us. It absolutely is the purpose of God for us to enter that place where we live under an open heaven, where reality is dictated not by fallen circumstances, but rather by heavenly mandate.

The tree that didn't bear fruit was cursed because God originally intended it to operate twelve months a year, 365 days a year… always fruitful…. always in season.

The generation that lives under an open heaven… expects to operate out of the mindset of the garden.

They have learned to live in the "redeemed" world, not simply cope with the fallen one. They have learned well that prayer of Jesus, "your will be done on earth JUST AS IT IS in heaven." They see themselves as crusaders of the purposes of Jesus on the earth, those who will liberate, free, and heal every facet of society, every facet of humanity, every facet of a sickly world, into the redemption of a Holy Restoring God!

1 Revelation 22:2

2. 2 Timothy 4:2

3. Titus 1:3

CHAPTER SIXTEEN

HOLY FRUSTRATION

he secret of spiritual success is a hunger that persists... it is an awful condition to be satisfied with one's spiritual attainments... God is and was looking for hungry, thirsty people." – Smith Wigglesworth

Everywhere I look, a phenomenon is happening in the lives of believers. There is a frustration, dissatisfaction, discontent, restlessness and weariness that is invading the lives of so many in so many facets of the church. What is going on? How come so many are experiencing this personal crisis in the midst of days where they are seeking Jesus more than ever, loving Him more than they ever have, and walking with Him daily?

Is this some sort of mass discouragement that is unfolding on the church?

" *So Jacob was left alone, and a man wrestled with him till daybreak. When the man saw that he could not overpower him, he touched the socket of Jacob's hip so that his hip was wrenched as he wrestled with the man. Then the man said, "Let me go, for it is daybreak." But Jacob replied, "I will not let you go unless you bless me." The man asked him, "What is your name?" "Jacob," he answered. Then the man said, "Your name will no longer be Jacob, but Israel, because you have struggled with God and with men and have overcome." Jacob said, "Please tell me your name." But he replied, "Why do you ask my name?" Then he blessed him there. So Jacob called the place Peniel, saying, "It is because I saw God face to face, and yet my life was spared." The sun rose above him as he passed Peniel, and he was limping because of his hip."*

Gen 32:24-31

The hunger is here!

The emerging Bride full of power is waking up! No longer are they satisfied to sleep through their destiny, no longer are they willing to sit through a game that everyone else plays. Finally, the day is dawning where God can use a people who have worked through all there fidgets, twitches, jiggles!

We have been like a little child sitting in a "grown up" meeting, resorting to counting tiles and playing with our

Father's watch waiting for Jesus to show up and reveal true love, power, revelation, and brilliance. Until that happens, most of us have been simply watching the clock... waiting for this part of the meeting to end...

The early church was much that way! Their frustration finally ended in a cataclysmic release of Power such as the world had never seen!

In Acts[1] we read the narrative of the final days of barrenness for the early church. The emotions and actions are so very real to so many of us who have been involved in ministry for any length of time.

Peter and the other disciples looked around the room and realized that there were only eleven disciples. Their understanding of scripture was clear that there should be twelve. The impulse was set in motion to fulfill the prophecy one way or another.

Peter responds, (as Peter usually does) with a quick solution to the problem of God not showing up! His answer reminds so much like our fidgeting. "Hey guys, I figured out what we need to do in order for the Holy Spirit to come! We need this guy to come here. He's been around Jesus, He's a good guy, great speaker, full of God. We need him to come and release this thing!"

Peter decides the "spiritual" (sic) thing would be to fill the role, regardless of the means. He decided on drawing straws. We are no different. We decide by polling congregations, leaders, and friends for the best "well known" speaker around.

I wonder if they ever watched Jesus DRAW STRAWS? I guarantee you they didn't! Is that how Jesus figured out how to do what the Father was doing? I don't think so. In this case the straws point to this poor guy Matthias who is never heard of in the Bible again!!! What a great idea Pete! Do you think maybe, just maybe the Father was waiting to introduce a "Paul?" It might seem a more credible appointment than one who would wear the title without a power encounter with the Risen Lord.

The overwhelming effect of the appointment was significant! Frustration increased. Nothing more happened! It didn't make things better in anyway in the early church.

Although the impulsive appointment didn't produce the outpouring, it did finally produce the end of exasperation! The end of our frustration is a "resignation" that unless God does this nothing will happen! The point of this surrender is the place God has always wanted us to be. It is there that God will release His Power.

It's almost like the Lord is saying to us, "Are you done yet? Have you done everything you know to do? Is there anything else you want to try to make this thing happen? Because as soon as you are done, I want to do something that will go way beyond your wildest expectations, something that can't be attributed to a man, or a denomination, or a movement. I want to pour out My

Spirit, and literally change the landscape that you have become so familiar with! As soon as you are done, we can get underway. As soon as you have reached the end of your frustrations. As soon as you have conceded and relinquished your way to make Me move. As soon as you have surrendered to me, to my timing, to my way, then the Glorious Bride, the Church that you have longed for, the Power that you have dreamed of, the Miracles that have eluded you will be released... and you will be known by My Name and My Movement and My Power!"

1. Acts 1:20-26

CHAPTER SEVENTEEN

THIS JESUS... THIS GENERATION

$\mathcal{L}$et this be written for a future generation, that a people not yet created may praise the LORD: The LORD looked down from his sanctuary on high, from heaven he viewed the earth, to hear the groans of the prisoners and release those condemned to death."

Psalms 102:18-20

It's now!

A generation is rising unlike any previous generation. It holds in its hands the keys of that which will unlock the heavens and release the storehouses of the miraculous prophesied by Jesus.

There never has been a generation that has seen "more than" Jesus saw. This generation is beginning to apprehend it! Heaven is becoming familiar with the faces of this generation as repeatedly they enter the Holy Place and invoke the Presence of God on the earth. This time the story is not about a "theological" answer for men... this time, it's about the raw Love and Power of God demonstrated in ways that will confound the scholar and make believers out of atheists! This generation lives differently, acts differently, sounds differently, and evidently is hearing differently than what its predecessors have heard!

In order to understand this generation... we must understand Jesus!

"Jesus gave them this answer: "I tell you the truth, the Son can do nothing by himself; he can do only what he sees his Father doing, because whatever the Father does the Son also does. For the Father loves the Son and shows him all he does. Yes, to your amazement he will show him even greater things than these. For just as the Father raises the dead and gives them life, even so the Son gives life to whom he is pleased to give it."

(John 5:19-21)

Only the fool would believe that they could produce what God wants. Jesus submitted His entire ministry and life to the timing and ways of the Father. His declaration of dependence was not simply a nice phrase that we can repeat in order to cause people to believe we are hearing something from God. The outworking of the Father in His life repeatedly evidenced his complete and total dependence on God.

Jesus lived out the "phrases" He spoke. His lifestyle was one of faith. When Jesus declared that we were "not to worry" and that God would take care of us, [1] he was not making a statement that would not be required of us, or of Him.

Faith revokes anxiety of any authority.

Although God had always provided for His children, there would be a new understanding of that provision in days to come. The provision of God during the Exodus is one of the most amazing miracles to ever come on to an entire generation. That generation experienced the operation of faith for forty years, and yet they never got it! They never entered into the rest that is provided through an active faith that sees the workings of God in all aspects of life. They may never have had "more than enough", but they always had "enough!"

This generation will also have "enough!" But they will recognize the value of proceeding in Faith. They will not simply witness the stories of others who walk in faith. They will not simply be able to recite the Biblical stories of those who went before them. These are those who themselves "walk on water."

These are those who see what the Father is doing… and demonstrate the Father's work. Just as a child learns to color between the lines, this generation sees the "outline" of what the Father is doing and fills in the "colors" to make the picture known!

We are a generation "undone" by His Presence and captured for His purposes, not to accomplish our destinies, but His! We have not simply counted the cost; we have experienced the sacrifice of the cost! We seek no fame but His! That His Name be exalted! That His Name be honored! That His fame be extended to the Nations until every knee bows, every tongue tells, both the lost and the found, in heaven and in hell, that Jesus Christ is Lord!

1.   Matthew 6:33

CHAPTER EIGHTEEN

APOSTOLIC LOVE ...
THAT COVERS NATIONS!

When the men rose up from there, and looked down toward Sodom; and Abraham was walking with them to send them off. And the LORD said, "Shall I hide from Abraham what I am about to do, since Abraham will surely become a great and mighty nation, and in him all the nations of the earth will be blessed? "For I have chosen him, in order that he may command his children and his household after him to keep the way of the LORD by doing righteousness and justice; in order that the LORD may bring upon Abraham what He has spoken about him." And the LORD said, "The outcry of Sodom and Gomorrah is indeed great, and their sin is exceedingly grave. "I will go down now, and see if they have done entirely according to its outcry, which has come to Me; and if not, I will know." Then the men turned away from there and went toward Sodom, while Abraham was still standing before the LORD.

Genesis 18:16-22

When God has to visit a place in order to see it, Apostolic Love has covered it! Often I have heard people say that Lot had no business living in Sodom. Some say he was a compromiser for living in a city with so much licentiousness and evil! 2 Peter 2:7 says Lot was a righteous man who was distressed by the world around him. His distress did not remove him from the city, but rather affected him in order to be light to those around him. It is obvious that Lot was touched by the hand of God to love those around him to the degree that his love for them "covered" their sins before God. In fact, so great was this covering of Love that God could not see the wickedness from heaven but had to come down to earth and find out the truth![1] Love covers a multitude of sin. I would venture to say that Apostolic Love covers the multitudes sins!

The foundation of "the restoration of all things" found in Acts 3:21 is intense love. It is only this profound love that can remedy the issues and problems of this world. The weapons we fight with are not of this world. The weapons we fight with are birthed out of love. It is love alone that will "pull down" those things that exalt themselves above God... into a place of brokenness, humility, and faith. All the ministry we do, all the training and equipping for the Harvest, is simply a gong without love! It was love that produced the most significant lasting fruit in any of the previous awakenings, and it is love that will produce that same result today!

Charles Grandison Finney, one of the most remarkable and effective revivalists of the 2nd Great Awakening had the most dramatic fruit that lasted of any revivalist! I believe it was his encounter with Jesus that made it that way.

> "I went to my dinner, and found I had no appetite to eat. I then went to the office, and found that Squire W- had gone to dinner. I took down my bass-viol, and as I was accustomed to do, began to play and sing some pieces of sacred music. But as soon as I began to sing those sacred words, I began to weep. It seemed as if my heart was all liquid; and my feelings were in such a state that I could not hear my own voice in singing without causing my sensibility to overflow. I wondered at this, and tried to suppress my tears, but could not. After trying in vain to suppress my tears, I put up my instrument and stopped singing....
>
> There was no fire, and no light, in the room; nevertheless it appeared to me as if it were perfectly light. As I went in and shut the door after me, it seemed as if I met the Lord Jesus Christ face to face. It

did not occur to me then, nor did it for some time afterward, that it was wholly a mental state. On the contrary it seemed to me that I saw him as I would see any other man. He said nothing, but looked at me in such a manner as to break me right down at his feet. I have always since regarded this as is most remarkable state of mind; for it seemed to me a reality, that he stood before me, and I fell down at his feet and poured out my soul to him. I wept aloud like a child, and made such confessions as I could with my choked utterance. It seemed to me that I bathed his feet with my tears; and yet I had no distinct impression that I touched him, that I recollect.

I must have continued in this state for a good while; but my mind was too much absorbed with the interview to recollect anything that I said. But I know, as soon as my mind became calm enough to break off from the interview, I returned to the front office, and found that the fire that I had made of large wood was nearly burned out. But as I turned and was about to take a seat by the fire, I received at mighty baptism of the Holy Ghost. Without any expectation of it, without ever having the thought in my mind that there was any such thing for me, without any recollection that I had ever heard the thing mentioned by any person in the world, the Holy Spirit descended upon me in as manner that seemed to go through me, body and soul. I could feel the impression, like a wave of electricity, going through and through me. **Indeed it seemed to come in waves and waves of liquid love; for I could not express it in any other way.** It seemed like the very breath of God. I can recollect distinctly that it seemed to fan me, like immense wings.

No words can express the wonderful love that was shed abroad in my heart. I wept aloud with joy and love; and I do not know but I should say, I literally bellowed out unutterable gushings of my heart. These waves came over me, and over me, and over me, one after the other, until I recollect I cried out, "I shall die if these wavers continue to pass over me." I said, "Lord, I cannot bear any more..."

Finney was impacted not by power, but by Love! It was this Love that compelled him to touch everyone everywhere with the Grace of Jesus. True Love always compels. It doesn't compel us to ministry, it compels us to serve. It doesn't compel us to accomplish, it compels us to ever increasing demonstrations of serving love to those around us. It is this kind of Love that overshadows a society in need of judgment, with grace and mercy!

During a profound encounter with the Lord Jesus after a major hurricane, I heard the Lord say there would be more events just as catastrophic. I asked Him if it was judgment. His powerful response burned in my spirit. He pointed me to the passage where Elijah witnesses the earthquake, the wind, and the fire in 1 Kings 19:11-12. *"So He said, 'Go forth, and stand on the mountain before the LORD.' And behold, the LORD was passing by! And a great and strong wind was rending the mountains and breaking in pieces the rocks before the LORD;* **but the LORD was not in the wind***. And after the wind an earthquake,* **but the LORD was not in the earthquake***. And after the earthquake a fire,* **but the LORD was not in the fire***; and after the fire a sound of a gentle blowing.'*

He spoke resoundingly to me. "Danny, I am not in the calamity... I am in the remedy!" Apostolic Love overwhelms the duty of God to bring judgment with the passion of God's Heart that every knee will bow in homage of Jesus! The world that doesn't know Jesus, already IS in judgment. Our task is to pull them from the place of judgment to the place of salvation! We are the "remedy of God" to reveal His Awesome Love to this world!

"For God did not send the Son into the world to judge the world, but that the world should be saved through Him. "He who believes in Him is not judged; he who

does not believe has been judged already, because he has not believed in the name of the only begotten Son of God. "And this is the judgment, that the light is come into the world, and men loved the darkness rather than the light; for their deeds were evil. "For everyone who does evil hates the light, and does not come to the light, lest his deeds should be exposed. "But he who practices the truth comes to the light, that his deeds may be manifested as having been wrought in God."

John 3:17-21

Historically, the church has prevailed with power on this world, not because of great speakers, not because of great churches and ministries, but because of someone, who like SOMEONE else (i.e. Jesus), had Apostolic Love and was willing to cover over in love the generation around them. 1 Peter 4:8 *"Above all, keep fervent in your love for one another, because love covers a multitude of sins."*

We must once again look at the darkest places not as places to avoid, but rather places to emphasize with His Light and His Love. These are the places requiring the most love; the Jesus kind of love that overshadows darkness with light! The communities immersed in sick bondage don't require the judgment of God, they already are experiencing it! Those communities and people groups require the love of those who have experienced that love… the people of God.

A couple years ago I was in San Francisco with a youthful ministry team. Early one Sunday morning on the way to a meeting we stopped at a café to get some coffee. As we walked through the door we were overwhelmed by the obvious fact that all in there walked in a homosexual lifestyle. One young man asked me if the Lord was showing me anything specific about anyone in the café. I indicated that He had shown me a number of things about individuals but I was not going to share them. He asked me why and I told him that I would tell him later. He responded that he had some words for someone, and asked if it would be okay if he shared with that individual. I told him that would be fine, knowing the response he would get. As he opened his mouth to speak, and began sharing specific things to a man in his twenties about his life, a hardness came into the young man in the bondage of a homosexual spirit and he angrily blurted out, "You're a preacher... a Christian... leave me alone!" He got up and left. As we left the café, my young apprentice asked me why I didn't share the things the Lord had shown me with anyone in the café? I simply told him, "They don't need words... they need love! It is only love that will redeem them from their judgment into salvation."

The church hasn't been called on to picket or curse. The church has been given the greatest power in the universe to bring about the most revolutionary change in the earth. It's not political, it requires no money, it requires no training... it simply requires having had an encounter with the Apostolic Lover of our Souls! It is this Gospel of Love that demonstrates true apostolic authority.

I don't give a rip about titles... show me love! Show me a laid down lover of Jesus... and I will show you a people around them who are falling in love with Jesus too! Undemonstrated love gives place to religious, stuffy, bureaucratic offices. Washing feet releases the heart of Him who is Love and demonstrates true apostolic love and true spiritual authority.

A dear friend of mine has been touching the poor for several years now. He is a businessman who buys the food without getting a tax write-off. He gives freely from his own resources. He is not looking for grants that require no sacrifice on his part. He wants to touch the hearts of people with love, not simply food! Recently he has been going into our city on Sunday afternoons to find the poor. His approach is revolutionary. He finds them to literally wash their feet. He wants to wash them with the love of Jesus. He wants to demonstrate this overwhelming love that saved him. The response has been amazing as these broken, trodden down, impoverished future "knee bowers" experience this love. Often the simplicity of that act, results in many hours of long ministry and healing. It sounds like Jesus to me!

When the waves of liquid love overwhelm us, waves of liquid love will flow through us! Until that time, we can't ask for our communities to change. We can't expect lives to be transformed. We will simply be a clanging gong...

The heart of the Lord is to raise up "righteous" servants in the midst of dark places. Those who don't run from darkness but rather bring light to it! Those who understand that purity is not affected or infected by association. True purity will allow a whore to wash your feet. True holiness and purity will allow you to take up the cause of a person caught in sin and point them to life! It is this apostolic love that when released will be the formation of the Greatest Awakening... where the fruit is not cast... and where the King finds a place to lay His Head!

It is this Love that both filled Jesus and continues to infect His disciples today. This Love releases the compassion, the mercy, the healing, the miraculous and the power to set generations free.

1. Genesis 18:21

CHAPTER NINETEEN

APOSTOLIC, LOW DOWN... LAID DOWN LOVERS!

O Jerusalem, Jerusalem, you who kill the prophets and stone those sent to you, how often I have longed to gather your children together, as a hen gathers her chicks under her wings, but you were not willing.

Matthew 23:37

I have become all things to all men so that by all possible means I might save some. I do all this for the sake of the gospel, that I may share in its blessings. Do you not know that in a race all the runners run, but only one gets the prize? Run in such a way as to get the prize. Everyone who competes in the games goes into strict training. They do it to get a crown that will not last; but we do it to get a crown that will last forever. Therefore I do not run like a man running aimlessly; I do not fight like a man beating the air. No, I beat my body and make it my slave so that after I have preached to others, I myself will not be disqualified for the prize.

1 Corinthians 9:22-27

For it seems to me that God has put us apostles on display at the end of the procession, like men condemned to die in the arena. We have been made a spectacle to the whole universe, to angels as well as to men.

1 Corinthians 4:9

Since all these things are to be destroyed in this way, what sort of people ought you to be in holy conduct and godliness, looking for and hastening the coming of the day of God, on account of which the heavens will be destroyed by burning, and the elements will melt with intense heat!

2 Peter 3:11-12

There is a release on the earth that is changing the lives and purpose of men and women from personal selfish aspirations into Godly men and women who will lay their lives down for the Gospel. We've had our heroes.... they speak at our conferences and declare the mighty works of God throughout the earth... but that is not all they have been doing. They have been releasing a Heavenly Jealousy for hearts that will be more passionate, more radical, more deeply consumed by the Love of Jesus than anything else. It is with such gratitude that I look on these forerunners, these front-runners... these who have touched heaven and brought it to earth. They have given me faith back! They have restored the passion and desire for Jesus that I lost while doing ministry and administrative tasks that seemed so important. They showed me that the God who I fell in love with as a child... who healed the sick, cleansed the lepers, and raised the dead is still alive and working in awesome power throughout the earth. They have demonstrated the sleepless nights of the early apostles.... the worn out bodies of those who traveled night and day to take the Kingdom where it had not been. They bear the marks of Jesus. They have been ridiculed and vilified by powerless nay-sayers who love their positions more than they love God or those that God came to reach! But still they press on.

They are reaching for an apostolic love that covers the nations. One that will plead with the Father for the lives of nations and the whole world. They press into a faith far beyond their ability... and yet they keep pressing. They laugh at danger, knowing the greatest victories lie in the most dangerous dark places! Every day could be their last. Every word that comes out of their mouths might be their final ones!

These are those who are the apostles who God is using. Crazy, wild, passionate servants of Jesus. They have looked into His eyes and everything in life changed!

They move by apostolic love! They are laid down lovers of Jesus! They remain low, unimportant, trivial in their passionate pursuit of an entire earth that will bow the knee to Jesus!

Apostolic love sees the one... lost... needing freedom... and desperate for a touch from God, even though they don't know it yet! Apostolic love looks past the sins of the city and sees the souls of the city. Apostolic love looks past the adulterer and says, "go your way, sin no more!" Apostolic love looks past perversion and darkness and says, "If God could show His love by sending His own Son to die for my sin, I surely will love you regardless of yours!"

The presence of righteous Lot in Sodom prevented judgment until he was removed! Would that Abraham had a greater faith that would have pressed into God and asked him to save the city for the sake of one!

The greatest and most holy mark of these water walkers is their love. Not simply spoken, but demonstrated. It is this love that will overwhelm nations, cities, towns, villages and communities. It is this love that will cause His Glory to cover the earth as the waters cover the sea. His Glory is Love. His Glory is demonstrated through Faith. And He Himself is the Hope of Glory!

Thank you heroes for inspiring my walk... but I must now look further! The Greatest... The Only... The Future for my life is You, Lord Jesus! Tell me to come to you... let me walk on water!

If you would like Danny Steyne or a Mountain Of Worship Team to speak at your church, ministry, or conference, or if you have interest in Mountain Of Worship, MOWBooks, MOWJournal, MOWMusic, MOWTeaching, MOWConferences, MOWSummits, MOWInternships, or Schools of Worship, Creativity, & Ministry, please contact us at the address below:

Mountain Of Worship

when true worshippers will worship

Mountain Of Worship
P.O. Box 212204
Columbia SC 29221-2204
803-665-8990
www.MountainOfWorship.com
worship@mountainofworship.com

In 1987 I had a vision. I saw a flat plain that grew into a volcano and became a "Mountain of Worship" that exploded worship all over the region, the nation, and around the world. It was an event of passionate worship that resulted in exaltation, magnification, and praise of God in spirit and truth! It was full of God's Power and the miraculous power of God was released to all those in the shadow of the Mountain. This "Mountain of Worship" is not simply another organization it is not simply another noun on the "marketplace" of Christianity ... it is an organism and a verb ... passionate about bringing Glory to the Father through "much fruit ... it is a "perpetual event of spirit and truth worship". It is a lifestyle of worship. It is a region... a nation... the world ... abandoned to passionate holy worship... until every knee bows, every tongue tells, both the lost and the found, in heaven and in hell... that Jesus is Lord!

Also available:

When Bruised Reeds Break
by Danny Steyne

~Returning a life to the Destiny God Intended~
A book on Restoration

"Danny Steyne's book, 'When Bruised Reeds Break,' is the best book for expressing the heart of God for broken people I have ever read...I was moved to tears as I read Danny's story...I highly recommend this book to every pastor, elder, deacon, and anyone else wondering about the heart of God and the issues pertaining to restoration." ~ **Randy Clark**

"To say this book is timely is a gross understatement. I trust that Danny's experience and message will be a wake-up call for our generation to mobilize and become a healing and restoring community. This book is invaluable for all..." ~ **Gary Oates**

"I write many endorsements, prefaces, and introductions and I do not recall many books to which I refer as a 'must-read.' But yours is one I would include in this short list of 'must reads'! ... I found a shallow and casual reading impossible...It is a story that, when read, touches all of us at some point of need, pain or fear." ~**Jack Taylor**

For more information on these and other MOW Products: please visit:
www.MountainOfWorship.com